The Philosopher Queen

Feminist Essays on War, Love, and Knowledge

103

Chris Cuomo

ROWMAN & LITTLEFIELD PUBLISHERS, INC.

Lanham • Boulder • New York • Oxford

ROWMAN & LITTLEFIELD PUBLISHERS, INC.

Published in the United States of America
by Rowman & Littlefield Publishers, Inc.
A Member of the Rowman & Littlefield Publishing Group
4720 Boston Way, Lanham, Maryland 20706
www.rowmanlittlefield.com

PO Box 317
Oxford
OX2 9RU, UK

British Library Cataloguing in Publication Information Available

Library of Congress Cataloging-in-Publication Data

Cuomo, Chris J.
    The philosopher queen : feminist essays on war, love, and knowledge / Chris Cuomo.
        p. cm. — (Feminist constructions)
    Includes bibliographical references and index.
    ISBN 0-7425-1380-7 (alk. paper) — ISBN 0-7425-1381-5 (pbk. : alk. paper)
    1. Feminist theory. 2. Feminism. I. Title. II. Series.

HQ1190 .C866 2002
305.42'01—dc21   2002009705

Printed in the United States of America

♾™ The paper used in this publication meets the minimum requirements of American National Standard for Information Sciences—Permanence of Paper for Printed Library Materials, ANSI/NISO Z39.48-1992.

FOR KAREN

Contents

Acknowledgments

These essays were written in the midst of many wonderful circles of affection, political passion, and intellectual exchange. Thank you first of all to my darling Karen, for loving support and inspiration (I apologize for not doing my share of the housework while completing this book). Thank you to my parents Peter and Bonnie Cuomo, whom I treasure, and to the amazing Cuomo clan. Thank you to my other families, including the Kutys and the Schlangers, and loving thanks especially to the little ones for their capacity to draw forth giggles and smiles in the unlikeliest times. Lessons learned in the company of the late Joan Schlanger shape these essays in many ways —I thank Joan for encouraging me to focus on writing.

Special thanks to my beloved Cincinnati family, who nurtured me though my time in the cave (especially Ursula Roma, Catherine Raissiguier, Lycette Nelson, Madeleine Pabis, Claralee Miller and Fran Haas, who read and discussed early versions of the work). Thank you to my families in Perth and Santa Fe, and to Vicky Davion, my philosophical sister. Patsy Hallen, dear friend and fairy godmother, has been a special source of inspiration. Ted Morris, lover of philosophy and music, is a foundational friend. Thank you to Amber Katherine for deep intellectual companionship (and a monk's retreat), and to Janna Richards for incredible techno-talent and generosity.

Thanks to Hilde and Sally Ruddick, editors of the Feminist Constructions series, Eve DeVaro and Rowman & Littlefield for supporting this project, and Andrea Reider for her excellent design work.

As much as I like to complain about the academic world, this work would not exist but for the support of several wonderful professional communities: The Society for Women in Philosophy (especially Midwest SWIP), Feminist Ethics and Social Theory (FEAST), The International Association of Women Philosophers, and the Society for Lesbian and Gay Philosophy. Thank you to all of the brilliant friends, colleagues, and teachers who provided feedback and illuminating conversation, especially the members of the Women's Studies Program at the University of Cincinnati, and Linda Martín Alcoff, Alison Bailey, Claudia Card, Laurie Fuller, Kim Hall, María Lugones, Bob Richardson, and Nancy Tuana. Thank you to the Department of Philosophy and the Dean of Arts and Sciences at the University of Cincinnati, for providing sabbatical and unpaid leave that allowed me to complete this book.

Thank you to my activist buddies, from Stonewall Cincinnati to SWIP to New Yorkers Say No to War. And thank you to all of my wonderful students at the University of Cincinnati and Murdoch University, for teaching me more than I wanted to know. Finally, thank you to Alx for dropping the letter.

To my dear Colleagues: Thank you for providing the practical and intellectual space I needed to write these essays. May they somehow persuade you that affirmative action principles and policies should be applied at the micro, as well as the macro levels.

✳ ✳ ✳

Some of these essays have been previously published, and some are revised versions of published material. All work is used with permission.

"The King of Whiteness" is from *Whiteness: Feminist Philosophical Reflections*, edited by Chris Cuomo and Kim Hall (Rowman & Littlefield, 1999). "Sisterwomanchainsaw" is from *Feminism and Ecological Communities: An Ethic of Flourishing* (Routledge, 1998). "Justice, Joy, and Feminist Sex" is based on "Feminist Sex at Century's End: Thoughts on Justice and Joy," in *Feminist Ethics and Politics*, Claudia Card, ed. (Lawrence: University of Kansas Press, 1999).

"Lesbian and Its Synonyms" includes excerpts from "Thoughts on Lesbian Differences," *Hypatia* 13(1): 198–205. Other parts of that essay were developed for a panel on sexual identity presented at the meetings of the American Studies Association, October 2000. Thank you to Mona Bachmann and Cheryl Chase for stimulating ideas and discussion.

"War as an Opportunity for Learning" includes excerpts from "Why War Is Not Just an Event: Reflections on the Significance of Everyday Violence," *Hypatia* 11(4): 30–45.

"Getting Closer: On the Ethics of Knowledge Production" was originally published on the website of the Harvard University Forum on Religion and Ecology. http://environment.harvard.edu/religion/research/ethcuomo.htm.

"The Philosopher Queen" is available in audio form at www.chriscuomo.org.

Introduction

There are so many reasons to despair. Then again, life can be awfully wonderful. Philosophy is supposed to help us negotiate a wild, wicked world, and to provide some understanding of being and existence. The best philosophy aims to promote the good and to produce knowledge, and therefore to enable flourishing.

Philosophy cannot help but dwell in the world of ideals, because it emerges through ideas about truths, which are by nature universal (though always also partial). Philosophy cannot help but be embodied, because all knowledge emerges through bodies who are in constant contact with other bodies.

This philosophy is about ethics. As a branch of philosophy, ethics asks questions about norms and values, and inquires about the good. All of these essays aim toward and investigate an ethical ideal, which I summarize in "Getting Closer," as *a better world, the good life for all, a smarter society, a healthier planet, a more sensual, arousing culture, a life-loving, peaceful, happy, clearheaded, okay world.* Do you find that silly and overly optimistic? The essay "Justice, Joy, and Feminist Sex" provides a fairly detailed discussion of the importance of ethics, and of realistic and idealistic theorizing about ethics. "Ethics, Earth, and the Secular Sacred" reflects on values and the power of choice.

This philosophy is political theory. It takes ethics and existence to be inextricably political, and about power. Seeing power as a function of the state, but more fundamentally as what is described by the phrase "the personal is political," these essays describe and analyze the workings of power. Most also recommend taking or acting on power in particular ways. This work is also political theory in the sense that it was written in conversation with a specific scholarly tradition and literature, in Philosophy and beyond, and in the midst of particular political events and realities. For example, I did not intend to write a book with an emphasis on war, but since so much of this writing was done in the shadow of 9/11 (and in New York City), the preoccupation could not help but shape my agendas. "War as an Opportunity for Learning" is an attempt to make sense from a particular and politically charged location. This philosophy is written by an activist.

This philosophy joins forces with art. Some of these essays were written to be spoken in front of an audience, with movement and music. I developed the character of the Philosopher Queen and the practice of stand-up philosophy because I found standard philosophical discourse and method inadequate for addressing the questions I see as central. (I also usually find them rather boring.) I am obsessed with contradictions and the spaces between dichotomies, and I find that my questions and insights about those zones are sometimes best explored through narrative, self-disclosure, and humor. The tools of Philosophy—its methods of argumentation and its sacred texts—are invaluable, but limiting myself to those tools feels like wearing a girdle. I love engaging an audience philosophically (a mutual engagement, at best), and I hope this work encourages other philosophers to find new ways to connect with communities beyond the pale world of our discipline.

This philosophy is feminist. In "Critical Theory and the Science of Complexity," I say that feminism asserts *a relatively simple empirical fact, coupled with a fairly simple ethical claim: social worlds tend to present inadequate options to women, categorically, and the conditions that enable and further that oppression ought to be eliminated or transformed.* I hope anyone who is down with that conception of feminism will feel welcomed as a feminist here. I also argue that what seems to be a simple description of reality is really not so simple, that feminism is complex, and fundamentally about race, class, sexuality, and species. In *"Lesbian* and Its Synonyms," I invite all feminists to reconsider the significance of lesbian reality for contemporary feminism.

This philosophy expresses hope for science. Essays on secular sacredness, war, complexity, and the ethics of knowledge production all hold out the belief that science can be put in the service of life. *Science can be a form of interaction with the world that brings us closer to what we hold sacred, and helps us gain the knowledge we need to protect what we love.*

This philosophy discloses my fantasy of the connections between theory and life. "Simone Weil: It's Better to Fade Away" indulges that fantasy, as do the narratives "Sisterwomanchainsaw" and "The King of Whiteness." The Philosopher Queen pieces thoroughly inhabit the fantasy that praxis can bring wisdom, and encourage joyful dance through a body that is earthly, social, and female.

This philosophy loves the earth. It emerges from my own desperate sense that we need to question our collective death wish (or *their* collective death wish, if you will). My ground-zero knowledge is that it is never too late to turn things around for the better.

The Philosopher Queen

I t was an exceedingly sunny day and the sky was blue blue blue. The Philosopher Queen lay on her back, face to the heavens, and allowed her mind to float. She recalled faces, phrases locked in her brain, and felt the taste of salt on her tight dry lips. How long had it been since she'd felt connected? Why were the wonderful moments so fleeting?

A line of sweat found her ass, tickling her.

She knew in the long run no one person really has much of an impact on the world. She sometimes felt she could barely sort out her own beliefs from the rhetoric she'd been singing for what felt forever.

The Philosopher Queen wondered if the theme of her current train of thought was *Democracy and Culture*.

She opened her notebook and wrote:

No matter where we sit in relation to power, we each one of us (and all of us together) have a right and responsibility to shape common cultures that are life-enhancing and not . . . hateful (?). In the 21st century, democracy and multiculturalism are inextricably bound.

She lay back down and wondered if she was burning, but she didn't shift or turn. The sun was transforming her, making her its own. Her

1

eyelids, her sports bra, and her baggy trunks were all that kept her from becoming one with the blazing sky.

Rehydration is the key to life, she thought as she sat up, gulped cool water and remembered where she was.

The Philosopher Queen was sitting on a beach. She was in the middle of the years before the middle of life. She had a Ph.D. in Philosophy and was employed full time, with tenure. She was on vacation, and trying to figure out if she hated her life.

Days like last Thursday made her think she could go on like this forever, for another twenty-five years. Her life was small, tucked into an unglamorous corner of reality, but she regularly experienced common luxuries and was lucky to know a pervasive absence of pain (knock wood). She was a teacher, and although teaching gave her headaches, it also allowed her to share clues and ideas with others. As a teacher, she developed a number of really good relationships of various sorts, with students and other teachers of various sorts. Sometimes when she spoke to a roomful of people about a topic that ignited her passions, they would pay close attention to what she said. She liked that, and these positive feelings associated with her everyday work made her feel lucky, and helped provide a rhythm in her life. Now she was wondering if this feeling had tricked her into believing her work was important.

Time for a swim! PQ jumped up, adjusted her straps, and bleary-eyed, walked toward the waves. The water was ice cold on her roasted paws.

Her brain became saltnumb as she surrendered to the certainty of the sea.

She thought she should try to get a different job, closer to . . . the sea, or some mountains maybe. What am I staying here for, my awesome career?

Professor LaLaFace
Chair, Center for the Study of Studies
Someplace Better, USA

Dear Professor Blankety-Blank,

Please accept this letter of application for your advertised position in
Feminist Theory. I am quite interested in the advertised position for a
number of reasons, but the most compelling is my desire to work in an
interdisciplinary context, and to contribute to the development of a program at the forefront of the study of Studies. I have much energy and
experience to offer such a program, and I know that my own work will
thrive in an environment that values interdisciplinary inquiry, and that
encourages teaching that is both rigorous and relevant.

Please, this job looks so cool and it's in the big city, where so many
of my friends live. Please just give me an interview and I know you'll like
me, either that or I'll find out that you and your people are a bunch of
freaks and I don't really want to work with you anyway. But it really
seems that my life would be just perfect if I lived there, instead of here,
and worked in your department, your institution, your discipline, instead
of mine. Please just call me, and do it soon. I'll do almost anything for an
interview. I am a desperate woman.

Cordially?
Sincerely yours?
Lotsa love?

The Philosopher Queen moved out of the water, sand sucking at her
strong ankles, the pull of the retreating tide begging her return to the
waves. Then just minutes later, it felt so nice to be back on her clean towel
on the malleable sand, hot and dry.

She was currently teaching an Intro course that included excerpts from *The Republic*. Suddenly she got the thought that she ought to feel guilty since she was lying on a beach and not getting any work done. And soon after that she began to actually *feel* guilty for lying on a beach and not getting any work done, so she decided to think about *The Republic* while laying on the beach. But instead of thinking about *The Republic* she thought about the first time she read *The Republic* cover to cover, when she was a student at a small college in upstate New York, away from everything she had known before. She remembered reading all those words, even the ones she didn't understand, and how she related to what she was reading, how she wanted to be in the puzzle. Wanting a piece of what was going on in that famous old book, she realized she was finally reading her favorite questions. She found Socrates completely convincing, as she was initially convinced by nearly everything she ever read in a philosophy class. Convinced until the next day when the impressive professor would provide the miraculous counterarguments, point out the holes, the hidden assumptions. Even in the face of ancient certainty, critical thought could transform conviction. And now look: here she was, a professional philosopher, a professional provider of counterarguments, a seeker of hidden assumptions, and wasn't that a thrilling life to be living at the beginning of a new century.

PQ felt the allover pinch of burning skin. Good, she thought, I need to shed. She reached again for her pen.

No, no it's not that I believed in the Philosopher King, I like democracy of course, I mean I benefit from it, don't I? But one can see the social need for an attentive, intelligent, and benevolent leader. A queen who gives voice to the oppressed. Who knows her role is to seek and promote truth (not necessarily to ever really find Truth). Who knows that now, on this planet (though of course not necessarily in every possible world), truth is the domain of the learned underclasses, dark and female.

Power can only shift through the command of power. No, that's not right, is it? In a world of teeming pluralities, negotiation can only go so far. A queen must seek, question, and command. Bring the peoples' knowledge, the earth's knowledge, to power.

Then again, she thought, questions about democracy and culture can only say so much about reality. The Philosopher Queen was a great fan of culture in the service of life and love, delighting in contradictions and ambiguities—products of history, land, sky, and sea. Human knowledge can never fully capture life, she thought. On some levels, people, flora and fauna, atoms and energies intermingle and relate in their own ways, on their own terms, regardless of the dictates of corporate government, regardless of what we write, what we say, what we know.

She started a list.

LIES I WAS TOLD IN GRADUATE SCHOOL:

1. The Mind

I have a new proposal for how to deal with dualisms. Let's just get rid of the nasty side of the equation. "Body" includes mind. But "mind" does not include body. So understanding and constructing the self/person/subject/will as rational is simply a too-narrow conception of human existence. Let's just stop pretending it's possible to know with a mind that is not also a body. Let's start a movement to just refer to the body and its knowing, and let's assume embodied knowing includes forms of knowing that coalesce in brains, and elsewhere as well.

Her stomach growled, and she smiled and reached for the Japanese rice crackers in her bag. They were crunchy and salt, and for a few minutes her whole world was the crunching in her mouth and ears, and secretions in her mouth and sinus cavities, and a satisfied belly amid more crunching and reaching for water and thinking about maybe eating fish for dinner.

PQ had big realizations. Sometimes they were frightening, or strange, or just wrong, so she'd learned to keep her mouth shut until the freshness wore off, her heart stopped beating so fast, and she'd had some time to sleep on the scary new idea. Was that why she'd initially been turned on by Philosophy?

When she first read Descartes, he had moved her to tears. A lover of drama, she was comforted by the knowledge that she was not alone in concocting evil genius, it's-all-a-dream fantasies. Transported through translations of seventeenth-century French and German, through arcane swirling England English, to the depths of Being, the heights of human possibility, as a young student, she'd felt high all the time. For hours, days, she could just wonder: What is existence? When am I going to get laid? Is a better world possible? Can justice be achieved? How on earth am I going to get my hands on some money?

She'd felt the questions immediately, was panicked and ill at ease until the blessed fleeting moment when she finally got ahold of her own opinions. But always, pressing at the base of her skull, was the other side of her obsessions: Her body. Laughter. The intrusions and magnetic pull of others. Why it is, how is it that so many people get so fucked over? Was it just a wicked world? Wouldn't it be good to have some understanding?

The Philosopher Queen loved to watch the sea, which was really watching the sea and the wind, and the movement of the earth and the play of the sun on the surfaces and depths of it all. And herself, looking through her own eyes but with the gaze of us, she in the many ways she was also we, seeing the sea, knowing the sea, naming the sea, because this is who she was. This is who we are, who we know ourselves to be.

PQ caught a glimpse of herself in the water and liked what she saw. Her brow was thick, her lips were fat. There were teenaged girls on the beach, more free, more confined than she'd been at their age. She remembered herself at thirteen, spending hours before the looking glass, in the brown and gold environment of the bathroom. Bare feet gripping the chocolate-colored bathmat, manicured hands gripping Formica, she'd lean across the sink and she'd look: The Horror!

No astringent could banish the blemishes. And the hairs! Above the lip, above the nose, beneath the chin, to pluck to bleach to scrub away. Eyes too droopy, cheeks too fat, Help me, *Seventeen* Magazine! Help me to accentuate my strengths and camouflage my sins. Give me peace of mind, make me clean. Fix me, Jesus, fix me.

She'd spent years in that room, scrutinizing and shaping. Transforming herself into something pretty and petite. A mutilating, modifying conversion experience, she'd had such success reproducing herself back then that sometimes even now she'd look at famous beautiful women and think *I could do that.*

Only books, and love, could break the spell of the looking glass. Only books, and love, could replace the mirror's ability to fill her days with the importance of improvement. Only books, and love, could bring the same buzzed satisfaction that came from the pursuit of a perfectly reflected self.

The Philosopher Queen wondered about Institutions of Higher Learning, and noticed the wisdom of a system that pulls lucky girls from their private mirrors and throws them into dorm rooms at the age of eighteen. Too much free time, too much available space in the head, and a girl could gnaw herself into a perfectly bleached and hairless skeleton.

But she had to tell the truth. It was not Descartes who brought her here. Not Descartes or Wollstonecraft or Beauvoir or Kant. It was The Gospel According to Mark. It was what happened when she read The Gospel According to Mark as a student of Philosophy. She'd spent her whole life knowing The Gospel According to Mark to be part of The Word of God. And then one wintery grey-cold day in upstate New York, she sat in a classroom listening to that really good professor discussing The Gospel According to Mark as a piece of something written by a particular man, in a particular social and historical location. She was listening and thinking and writing notes and maybe there was a cup of coffee on her desk as she considered The Gospel According to Mark as a piece of human writing, and not The Word of God. And at some moment that really felt like a moment, like an event, a solid weight of realization that felt like I HAVE BEEN LIED TO MY ENTIRE LIFE crushed her composure and stopped her pen. Her heart beat so loud everyone in the room could hear it. Trembling and burning out of her skin, she gathered her books and ran out of the classroom, and out of faith.

Her feet sunk into the wet sand as the edge of the ocean flowed up, and then away.

She looked down and saw a body that was her own and not her own. PQ felt just fine about what she saw. She felt proud that she provided a service to other members of her gender. Though she wasn't thin, she wore her bathing suit in two pieces. Though her teeth were not so white and her breath was not always fruity and fresh, she laughed with an open mouth, and spoke closely when the moment demanded it. Though her nipples were large and her breasts hung pendulous, she usually declined to wear a bra. She thought it good to offer other women the opportunity to look at her and know *if she can do it, then so can I.* And this all made her feel quite beautiful.

She looked down and saw a body that was her own and not her own. She looked from a perspective that was her own and not her own. She thought, I'm a social self, a discursive self, so why do I feel so alone? She confessed: Would I really have it any other way?

PQ put on another layer of clothing, punched sand into dips and hollows to accommodate her own, and lay face down on the bright beach towel. The gulls had found the rice crackers and their squawking competed with the nonsense in her head. Each squawker indistinguishable from the next, scratching for food, trying to be the loudest. I wish I was a bird. Breathe. Clear the mind. I can't stand these birds.

Wings on wind and fresh salty air and heat on the back of the head with thoughts that are insane and then full into nothing, and then a dream. . . .

You're standing at the front of a classroom. That guy Joe who always has his hand up is sitting right in front, looking expectant, waiting to see what you're going to do. Leelah, you like her but it's like pulling teeth to get her to talk in class, she's sitting in front too, but she's turned around, talking to the woman behind her. The classroom is full but these are the only two faces you know, and it feels like your mother is there. Not your mother but someone like your mother, an older woman who understands you, who knows you, who has helped you along. Maybe she's not even there, but you feel that kind of presence. And you start talking about birdcages, and you make a list on the board, a list you've written so many times before it's even accurate in your dream. The list says: mold, immobilize, reduce; internalize; constitutes groups; benefits those with power; systemic and systematic network of forces. And you're hitting the board and screaming out that list and you really want to be dramatic so you stride to the back of the classroom where you finally notice the faces back there and they're not familiar but they are distinct, and they're looking at you and you think, What am I doing? What have I done? And you remember your list on the board and when in doubt you can always go back to whatever you last wrote on the board. But from the back of the classroom you look and see that above the list you've written not the word *oppression*, the usual heading that you've written above this list for years now. Instead you've written the word THEORY, all in capitals and with a line underneath. Your heart starts beating so loud everyone in the room can hear it. You're trembling and burning out of your skin. But then you remember to laugh, and you wake up laughing, giggling wildly inside your experience, though on the outside the seagulls only hear a sleepy human chuckle.

The Philosopher Queen reached into her bag and grabbed her cards. She sat cross-legged, erect, and breathed deeply as she shuffled the deck, like a casino dealer, like her dad playing poker. Then she stopped and thought for a moment about water. About the beautiful immense omnipotent ocean, and about how good it felt to have a drink of water while hanging out here on the beach. She took a gulp of water (rehydration is the key to life), and shuffled the cards. The sun was behind her, casting shadows in the sand. She felt the heat on her shoulders and smiled at the illuminated world around her. She thought, even in winter in upstate New York it's the sun that keeps us warm and alive, as she shuffled the cards.

Air. She took a deep breath and felt her body. Kept breathing and noticing her breathing and thought, I wish I could quiet my mind. Breathe. Breath is the key to a calm and focused mind. And she gave the cards a shuffle. Then she wiggled her hips until she sat right on the earth. Yes, it's a wonderful planet, a wonderful place, she nearly said aloud as she nodded, and shuffled the cards again.

I am so weird, she thought. I think my problems are such a big deal. I think I am so important. I appreciate my own spirit, and I hope I can use these self-obsessions to do good work in the world. Look at those silly seagulls. She shuffled the cards one last time, while she thought of the people she loved. With her left hand she placed the deck face down on the sand, cut the deck, and restacked the deck. She turned over the top card and revealed the Two of Swords.

Mental Balance. Calm. A woman standing at the edge of the sea, her body supple, her mind alert. Standing in the pose of the bird who stands beside her. Balanced. PQ thought perhaps balance is an intellectual virtue, and she imagined the members of the Department of Philosophy, sitting around their table, declaring, Ah yes, that certainly was a *balanced* argument, wasn't it, Dick? What a fine philosopher, awfully *balanced* in his approach!

PQ decided to introduce the concept of balance when she next visited their world of Philosophy.

The Philosopher Queen was thinking about bubbles. All edge and reflection. Like social spaces. Like people. Sometimes the presence of an edge, or a boundary, is enough to convince us that something is really there. Nation, body, family, race. . . .

And it's there, isn't it? Just cross the border and you'll find out how real that bubble is. Won't you?

And now you are walking on the beach. You are walking toward that same spot, because you are her lover, and because you are the Philosopher Queen. The Philosopher Queen lies with her head in her lover's lap and feels her strong fingers stroking her weary scalp. She is confused about edges.

War as an Opportunity for Learning

1.

Philosophical engagement with matters of war includes work on what war is, and arguments about the conditions under which war is justified. But philosophers also engage war more directly, and use philosophical analyses to investigate particular wars. In 1966 and 1967, Bertrand Russell organized War Crimes Tribunals with the objective of deciding whether the United States (and South Korea, New Zealand, and Australia) was committing war crimes in Vietnam, and to "prevent the crime of silence" regarding military atrocities. Jean-Paul Sartre was also an active participant and contributed an insightful essay on genocide to the proceedings. While it could be argued that an international forum of civilian intellectuals can only draw symbolic conclusions (their conclusion was that war crimes were perpetrated in Vietnam), the tribunals provided information and analysis and made visible a fundamental relationship between philosophical engagement and struggles for justice. War is serious moral business, and philosophy refuses to take war lightly.

Philosophy about war is not the only philosophy to emerge from war. War and suffering demand philosophical attention, but they also sharpen our awareness of all aspects of politics, ethics, and existence. Philosophy traces connections between international wars and other expressions of violence and power, and by mapping out and analyzing relevant histories and military realities. In 1995 I participated in an international philosophy conference on war—a standard meeting of academics presenting papers and wandering around town in search of a nice place to eat dinner. We were not in the media spotlight, and no one was awaiting our grand conclusions, but it felt as though our conversations and investigations were timely and important. The realities of war in Bosnia-Herzegovina, including mass rape and genocide, were still reverberating, and it had just hit the news that three U.S. servicemen stationed in Okinawa were accused of raping a twelve-year-old Japanese girl. In conference sessions on the relationships between war and sexual violence, we discussed the deep assumptions that enable and encourage such abhorrent acts and practices, and the relationships between hegemony and brutality. The philosophers in attendance included scholars from Eastern Europe who told of the destruction they had recently witnessed, and who described what it was like for one's identity to shift from tenured professor to war refugee.

There were many recent events that demanded serious theoretical attention. Indeed, it seemed that even the norms of international war, and therefore our basic understanding of what war *is*, were undergoing monumental changes. Philosophers were reflecting on what wars in Bosnia-Herzegovina, Rwanda, and the Persian Gulf had illustrated about technology, genocide, and rape as weapons of war. War-caused migrations of people, borders, and loyalties were creating new forms of identity and nation, and scholars asked what forms of international and human rights law could effectively address those realities, and what governing bodies might enforce them. We looked at recent global conflicts and considered which strategies for pursuing peace had been most effective, and why had they worked.

The conference took place in Vienna and was organized by the International Association of Women Philosophers. This was my first time visiting that part of Europe, and perhaps because I'd gone there to discuss war, I found it impossible not to be a Nazi-obsessed American tourist in Austria. I don't think it was just me—near the fiftieth anniversary of its end, nostalgia about WWII seemed omnipresent. In comparison to more recent wars, such as Vietnam and the "postmodern" Gulf War, WWII was com-

monly portrayed in the media as a perfect example of an old-fashioned justified war. It was also a strong symbolic presence at the philosophy conference,
because so many of us had been influenced by the work of European
Jewish intellectuals, French existentialists, and other postwar writers.

Although this was a gathering of philosophers, our engagement was
interdisciplinary. Many of us shared an interest in feminist social scientific
work on women and war, which has repeatedly shown how understanding
war requires investigating the inter-relatedness of colonialism, economy,
militarism, gender, and sexuality. War always involves power and physical
destruction, but new forms of war emerge from specific complex circumstances. The meanings of war are therefore historical and particular, but
also universally symbolic. We were interested in histories of particular
wars, but also in the deep meanings and mechanisms of all war. We
addressed nuclear wars and wars against women, and attempted new ways
of theorizing and approaching war. War was engaged as a form of existence, a metaphor, and a gendered, cultural practice.

Regarding war, a community of philosophers saw the need for deep
and complex thinking and strategizing, and for updated definitions of the
thing itself, so as to effectively promote peace.

2.

In September 2001, just a few days after the attacks on the World Trade
Center and the Pentagon, a top Bush aide declared that "we need new constructions of war." The U.S. was officially using poststructuralist language
to initiate a new form of war in response to a new sort of enemy, but it
wanted an old-fashioned war as well. The hasty call to war, heard before
anything was known about the perpetrators of the attacks, was spun as
responsiveness to a widespread need for revenge and a sense of control in
the face of terrorism. But one man's act of terrorism is another man's act of
war. There was no space for asking if the 9/11 suicide attackers believed
they were at war with the U.S., or if such a war had been declared. If the suicide bombers were participating in a war, were they also terrorists? Such distinctions were relevant, because in labeling the attacks on American civilians

"terrorism," strategic fact-finding was mostly irrelevant. The only strategy available was annihilation, because we do not negotiate with terrorists.

It is hoped that military responses will deter further violence, or sufficiently damage the enemy to make further violence impossible. Judgements about the most effective forms of deterrence and destruction require careful evaluation and consideration. When war is pursued as an automatic response to violence, a primary motivation is revenge. After the bombing of New York there were no public discussions of strategic responses to terrorism, no diplomatic offers that did not assume a state of war, no immediate plans to use America's incredible economic power to effect long-term change in the repressive and poverty-stricken nations where terrorism flourishes. Revenge was assumed to be a legitimate state response to mysterious but absolutely catastrophic violence. The desire for revenge may be legitimate, or so deeply engrained and encouraged that questions about its moral legitimacy are moot, but the strategic wisdom of revenge is never a given.

Big Media never questioned the belief that immediate military action was necessary to re-establish American security after such destruction on our soil, or that a dramatic display of military force was the best way to prevent further harm to American civilians and property. Hunger for revenge is a hunger for violence that could not have been satisfied by an ideological "cold" war against terrorism, because revenge for suffering and loss of life requires a real war—a war that causes suffering and loss of life. What revenge *can* re-establish is one's sense of oneself as capable and strong. Unfortunately, revenge does not alleviate suffering, or fill up the pit of loss that is born from brutal violence.

War requires enemy nations—people and land that can be justifiably destroyed. "Terrorists" were the enemy, but since terrorists are hidden, they do not make good military targets. Connections between the suicide hijackers and the Taliban leaders of Afghanistan provided a suitable target for revenge, and good reasons for waging a high-tech war against a clearly tyrannical regime (even though that misogynist regime and its terrorist training camps had been supported by the U.S. for years). But whether or not the war in Afghanistan satisfied desires for violence, the elimination of the Taliban or a particular fanatical religious leader could not be tanta-mount to the removal or reduction of threat—that other thing war is sup-posed to accomplish—because the threat of terrorism is absolutely diffuse.

To enable an American war against the elusive enemy *terrorism*, a shell-shocked and compliant U.S. Congress increased the power of an appointed President and relinquished their own constitutional role in guiding military affairs—it seems they thought a new form of war required a new form of government. But who exactly was the new and potentially omnipresent mil-itary enemy? A 1996 U.N. resolution defined terrorism as "criminal acts intended or calculated to provoke a state of terror in the general public, a group of persons, or particular persons, for political purposes." The U.S. vir-tually declared war on any nation that supports terrorists, but certainly not all terrorists are harbored by nations, and since the U.S. has funded terrorist groups in the past, such a declaration is clearly not meant to be universal. Even if the line between terrorists and nations could be drawn, or if it were possible to distinguish good terror-provoking criminals from bad ones, it would be difficult to proceed with a war on terrorism that was not somewhat arbitrary. As we have seen with the war on drugs, a war against dangerous and wealthy international criminals is a difficult war to wage, especially if the criminals are nationals of states run by crooked governments who do not officially support their crimes, but who clearly profit from their crimes.

An American war on terrorism is also unusual because the enemy includes Americans. The FBI defines domestic terrorism as "the unlawful use, or threatened use, of violence by a group or individual based and operating entirely within the United States (or its territories) without for-eign direction, committed against persons or property to intimidate or coerce a government, the civilian population, or any segment thereof, in furtherance of political or social objectives." Such a vague and wide-rang-ing definition of the enemy can justify the use of extensive deadly force against American protestors who throw rocks or break windows. There is no disputing that the most damaging and horrific example of domestic terrorism was the 1995 bombing of the Murrah Federal Building in Oklahoma City by right-wing fanatics trained by the U.S. military. Nonetheless, in a statement made before the Senate Select Committee on

Intelligence in 2002 (which included the definition of domestic terrorism provided above), Dale L. Watson, Executive Assistant Director of the FBI's program on Counterterrorism and Counterintelligence, focused on "ecoterrorism" that includes only the destruction of property:

> During the past decade we have witnessed dramatic changes in the nature of the terrorist threat. In the 1990s, right-wing extremism overtook left-wing terrorism as the most dangerous domestic terrorist threat to the country. During the past several years, special interest extremism—as characterized by the Animal Liberation Front (ALF) and the Earth Liberation Front (ELF)—has emerged as a serious terrorist threat. The FBI estimates that ALF/ELF have committed approximately 600 criminal acts in the United States since 1996, resulting in damages in excess of 42 million dollars.

Even if those numbers were accurate, they pale next to the billion-plus dollars lying executives at WorldCom cost state pension funds in 2002, and that's just a fraction of the losses caused by corporate malefaction. Remember that terrorists are targets of *war*, not police action. The American war on terrorism provides a paradigm for any regime that wants to address aggressive dissidence with military response, and it therefore threatens democracy everywhere. A war on terrorism identifies an omnipresent and diaphanous enemy and directs an unprecedented amount of cultural power and deadly and expensive technology toward its destruction. It is as open-ended as a war without end.

3.

In September 2001 many Americans learned that what felt like peace was not so simple, and that there are many places around the world where people feel they are at war with the U.S. In some versions of this war, anti-American rhetoric is used to promote fundamentalism and to curtail the flowering of human freedom (in the same ways that violent fundamentalists in the U.S. use xenophobia to rally their own sheeplike troops). But the seeds of violent anti-American sentiment have also been sown through the exploitative and brutalizing effects of American interests themselves (for an excellent discussion see Chalmers Johnson's *Blowback: The Costs and Consequences of American Empire*). As Palestinian activists are fond of saying, when people are attacked with weapons that are "Made in the USA" (literally or figuratively) how can they not regard the U.S. as an enemy?

Even supporters of the widescale military mission of the United States can see that people around the world have good reason to identify the U.S. with greed, violence, and other evils. The ethical and political questions raised by this reality are profound: How does American freedom rely on the enslavement of others? What are our moral responsibilities in relation to such inequitable symbioses? We are usually too wimpy or busy to directly think about such questions very often, but people tend to get more philosophical when they are at war.

The extent to which you feel that you at war depends on your proximity to war, and proximity can be a matter of physical or affective distance. War is partially a matter of consciousness. How many Americans felt we were at war while our tax dollars were funding the Contras in Nicaragua in the eighties? Who felt we were at war during the O. J. Simpson trial? Who feels that we are at war now?

War can teach us about the point of view of the other. After the September 11 attacks on the U.S., people of color reported time and time again that the experience of being terrorized was nothing new to them. Some anti-establishment radicals were humbled to learn how patriotic or prejudiced they felt upon learning of the attacks. People with privilege remarked that they had learned quite a lot about what it feels like to be targeted for no good reason. I heard a number of non-Muslim Latinos and African-Americans joke that it almost seemed like a relief to have the attention of racial profiling and racialized violence focused on someone else for a change. Arab-Americans and South Asians, who have been severely and systematically harassed by federal agencies since the attacks, protested racial profiling and immigrants' rights in ways that would not have been likely if the victims of harassment were still mostly Latino and Black.

A common refrain among all kinds of good-hearted Americans is that "now we know" something important. What do we know, and how can we amplify the life-affirming aspects of that knowledge? How can we make the most of the knowledge enabled by war, and prevent it from decaying into resentment and more violence?

4.

Military decisions are not the clean moral problems described by classical philosophers of war, such as Grotius, Augustine, and Aquinas, or by contemporary proponents of "just war" theories. Just war theories take wars to be isolated, definable events with clear boundaries that distinguish the circumstances in which standard moral rules and constraints, such as rules against murder and unprovoked violence, no longer apply. Just war principles are applied in proper decision-making by agents of the state before wars occur, or in looking back and evaluating wars and military actions once they are over. They therefore assume that military initiatives are distinct events. But in fact, declarations of war are usually overdetermined escalations of preexisting conditions. Just war criteria do not encourage evaluations of military and related institutions, including peacetime practices and how they relate to wartime activities. They cannot adequately address the ways armed conflicts between and among states emerge from omnipresent and violent state militarism, or the remarkable resemblances between states of peace and states of war.

Spatial metaphors (*in* war, *out* of war, *at* war) represent war as a separate, bounded sphere, and indicate the assumption that war is a realm of human activity vastly removed from normal life—a sort of happening that is appropriately conceived apart from everyday events in peaceful times. At the same time, war is also taken to be a necessary state that is inherent in human nature, that inevitably erupts and reconfigures reality. When war is seen as a necessary event, peacetime military practices enjoy immunity to moral reproach, because they too are considered necessary. Whether or not it is inevitable, *war is not just an event*, because it is a presence, a constant white noise in the background of social existence. It sometimes moves closer to the foreground of collective consciousness in the form of declared wars and documented violence, but it is always present in the form of everyday military violence. Neglecting the omnipresence of militarism allows the false belief that the absence of declared armed conflict is peace, the polar opposite of war. It is particularly easy for some of us to maintain this false belief, because privilege or luck or ignorance allows us to keep our distance from war.

Seeing war as an event is like seeing rape or school shootings or suicide bombings as isolated events rather than as occurrences that arise from specific social systems and values. When we take those things to be isolated events, we focus on evil men, insanity, and our own sense of powerlessness and pathos. Focusing on catastrophic events, movements against war or other forms of brutal violence are exercises in crisis control. Antiwar resistance is mobilized when the "real" violence occurs, or when the stability of privilege is directly threatened, and it seems necessary to drop all other political priorities. When the war is over, there is simply no longer a need for a movement (and we find that preexisting movements against violence and injustice have abated because everyone has been so distracted by the crisis of war).

But horribly damaging state-sponsored violence occurs regularly and widely, and much of it is perpetrated by military institutions and other militaristic agents of the state. Those institutions and agents are not just out there somewhere.

5.

The whole world comes to me in the form of dust.
Breath is our deepest relation with the world.
Every breath is a gulp of particulate
matter. Their bodies turned to dust.
That night black powder glittered in the street light.
If it is small enough it lands in your lungs.
I asked for a visit from peaceful spirits.
Dust more friendly than a mushroom cloud.
Floating ash is everywhere these days.
She said they'd bombed rubble into dust.
It's amazing what the body can handle.

6.

War is notorious for giving free rein to destruction and selfishness, but it also gives free rein to the imagination. Perhaps that is why strange couplings occur during war: Tony and María, Aimee and Jaguar, Rosie and Riveting, the Yankee and the Asian Beauty. Wars help focus the attention. People seek out information during war. They read the paper, talk about current events, check the Internet and listen to the radio. They formulate opinions and become aware of people and places that have only been invisibly relevant before.

Or they don't. Many people choose to stay away from the news during wartime, believing things like "I will get depressed if I pay attention to the news," or "I don't trust the news." If those beliefs are true, is their willful ignorance blameworthy?

Times of crisis bring awareness of our vulnerability and interdependence. It is unnerving to realize how much we rely on contingent institutions for information, protection, and administration, especially if we have trouble trusting them, or if we believe that part of their agenda is to serve elite interests. Because things can be so unpredictable, it is probably healthy to feel a little paranoid during wartime. But it is nearly impossible to make wise choices once paranoia has gotten the best of you.

War makes evident the need for real alternatives to war, and can therefore draw the imagination toward dreams of peace. When unspeakably bad things come into consciousness, for those who are physically safe there are moments when it appears that anything is possible, and so fantasies of a world beyond war become more clearly articulated. In thinking of alternatives to war, the imagination constructs alternatives to militaristic economies and symbolic systems, to imperialist values and institutions. War opens the space for fantasy and clarifies the wisdom and courage required for peace. Yet those fantasies make evident the immensity of the project of peace, and how far far we are from a world without war. The task of realizing peace is too daunting and requires too much cooperation, so we abandon the vision.

The pacifist refusal to let go of the ideal of peace is a lesson in moral courage. The warrior for peace bravely engages the unrealistic and asks embarrassing questions. Is the state a healthy form of human life? Is capitalism? What alternative collective bodies will promote the well-being of people and life on earth, and how will they do so without creating or relying on military threat?

Breathing is Human. War is not Human.

7.

In recent years, it has been instructive for Americans to witness activism against the presence of U.S. military bases in Vieques, Okinawa, Panama, and many other places. How many Americans could deal with living near a military base that housed 25,000 foreign soldiers? The fact that our security is thought to require the maintenance of thousands of military bases all over the world is not often in the American consciousness. Cynthia Enloe's classic *Bananas, Beaches, and Bases: Making Feminist Sense of International Politics* shows how dramatically American bases affect local economies and cultures, and especially the lives of women who service and support soldiers as prostitutes and wives.

War is a foundational trope in the social and political imagination, and the image of the warrior shapes gender everywhere. The warrior is not a natural necessity, but where identity requires violence, war is inevitable. Where masculinity is marked by violence, warriors become rapists. The warrior identity becomes a fetish when he is the only surviving model of masculinity. Colonialism, poverty, and female weakness have created a wide world of dangerous warriors.

But the warrior is complex, because along with the capacity for violence, the warrior symbolizes strength, security, and self determination. Security is necessary for survival, as autonomy is necessary for flourishing. Our needs and desires for security are not trivial or benign. But military-style policing and other forms of police brutality irrevocably undermine the fundamental trust in law that is necessary for democracy. Where the law itself systematically undermines the people's sense of security, there is a crisis in democracy. This world requires warriors, but where are the warrior-protectors, the warrior-resistors who do not require the counterpoint of woman-as-vessel, who do not romanticize or worship violence, who do not consider war to be law, and law to be an excuse for more war?

8.

American ingenuity: Proposal for a global campaign: Just Say Si!

Black T-shirts, words in red, green, and purple (work some white in there for better visibility?). Target Muslims, Christians, Jews, small towns, "inner cities" (other hothouses of violence?). Mothers get kids to take the pledge—especially boys. Like just say no, but cool. Invite Lauryn Hill and Snoop Dogg to do angry anthem . . . can we get a Pepsi tie-in? Set up *sports teams*. Kids turn over guns, bomb-building materials, military gear in exchange for educational opportunities, a gift bag of freebies.

Just say yes to life—to not blowing yourself or anyone else up for glory or god. What a concept!

9.

It is difficult to find reliable information about war during war. In the wars in Grenada and Panama, the U.S. established norms of drastic censorship that came to full effect in the Persian Gulf War. Now war reports are provided by military media managers, and Big Media has been exposed as just another corporate interest. No wonder so many otherwise level-headed people are attracted to conspiracy theories these days. *When we have to be in the business of filtering our own news, sharp evaluative tools and critical thinking skills are crucial.* Intrepid seekers scan the Internet and other corners for scraps and statistics, and when we are lucky the efforts bubble up and into consciousness. A professor in New Hampshire keeps track of civilian casualties in Afghanistan: www.cursor.org/stories/civilian_deaths.htm. An occupational psychologist in Great Britain investigates the use of depleted uranium in hard target smart bombs: Search *mystery metal*.

Any space that can disseminate information is also a good space for organizing. A group of New York City activists, artists, and academics use the Internet to create a ground-zero movement for peace: www. nysaynotowar.org.

Overall, the data is pretty clear: War is bad for children and other living things. An early illustration of the connections between the war on nature and our wars on each other was made by Rachel Carson in the first few pages of *Silent Spring*, where she describes insecticides as the offspring of World War II chemical weapons research. From insecticides to agribusiness to GMOs—military values even helped kill off the family farm.

A healthy and flourishing natural world is the most basic and promising interest that human beings share. But it has been difficult for peace activists and anti-nuke environmentalists to adjust to post-cold-war politics. Little did anyone realize how swiftly and easily global comprehensive bans, treaties, and moratoria could be reversed. American environmental groups tend to lie low (or roll over) during international conflicts, and they certainly do not emphasize the disastrous ecological effects of rampant militarism. But the natural world is the setting for all war, and all rehearsal and preparation for war. Natural noncombatants are everywhere, and their destruction is necessary for war and for the everyday existence of military institutions. Virtually all of the world's thirty-five nuclear bomb test sites, and most radioactive dumps and uranium mines, are on aboriginal land. If we took nature and human rights into account, we could rarely justify war. In *Scorched Earth: The Military's Assault on the Environment*, military veteran William Thomas chronicles the ecological realities of war and militarized peace. The U.S. military is the largest generator of hazardous waste in America, generating a ton of toxic pollution a minute, every day (and much more, of course, when we are "at war"), and more toxins annually than the world's top five chemical companies combined. And this is no secret—of 338 citations issued by the Environmental Protection Agency in 1989, three quarters went to military installations. The amount of resources required for routine military operations is staggering. In less than an hour, a military jet burns as much fuel as a North American motorist burns in two years.

10.

There were two things that they felt. First, they felt irrational fear. This was new for them, because they were not the kind of people who characteristically gravitated toward irrational fear. They were the type who say shut up, don't be crazy, don't even go there, what are you worrying yourself silly over? So it was surprising to them—these random fears that would bubble up out of nowhere, out of boredom or thought or implication. They feared they'd been nuked, that there had been some mysterious radioactive material in the suitcases. They felt like something else *very bad* was going to happen. They worried about the water, about the subways, about all the crazies they had learned to live with, about everyone who was going to misunderstand and hurt them again. They couldn't trust anything, and because almost everything in their lives depended on trust, their fear was cast as a bottomless pit of anxiety.

The second feeling was related to fear. In this new sense of pervasive panic, they really felt they were the center of the universe. Everything seemed related to them, to boil down to them, to what they were thinking and feeling, how they were affected, and what it might mean for them in the end. They were the only measure of reality that concerned them. They became even bigger drama queens, holding truth and a stiff drink in one hand and desperate love in the other.

Not all of the time of course, not even most of the time. But they did feel awful and strange, even though most of them had been safe at home when it happened. They were embarrassed to admit how off-balance it made them, because they had always thought of themselves as more solid than others, more capable of handling difficulty. But there were no words for the bottomless grief of knowing death. They had changed forever.

Some of them realized that if they moved all the way into these feelings, they might find something useful on the other side. *On the other side of fear are all the things I love. I breathe, and hold them in my mind and my heart, and try to be good to them.*

High-tilt self-centeredness was more difficult to spin into something positive. That felt like the white ego on drugs. But then again, there is something useful in being reminded that you are the center of your universe. We hear all the time that we are "connected to everything," but we don't usually feel so connected. Self-centeredness includes the realization that you are valuable, and it illuminates the lines drawn directly from all things to you. In self-centeredness you have a stake in everything, and you want it all, on your terms. This wanting can express itself in ugly grasping, but it also emerges from the sense that the world is a wonderful thing, a thing to grasp close to your heart.

If it is possible to separate the grasping ego from the love of the world, even just sometimes, the love of the world moves us forward. *In the yellow pit of fear, love was the only thing that calmed me. Then laughter. And after laughter, perhaps a thought about justice.*

11.

The U.S. is a war innovator. A culture that dedicates so much of its resources to the business of waging war cannot help but be a war innovator, because an economy that depends on weapons production and military supremacy must be obsessed with the continual improvement of war-making. The Center for Defense Information, a nonpartisan organization founded by former military personnel (www.cdi.org), reports that the U.S. military spends $589,802 every minute, doing business with top defense contractors including Lockheed Martin, Boeing/McDonnell-Douglas, Raytheon Company, General Dynamics, Northrop Grumman, The Carlyle Group, and General Electric. When American political leaders are major stockholders in these corporations, foreign and military policies are driven by the myth that war is "good for the economy."

Romantic conceptions of science and the pure pursuit of knowledge are dashed to bits when one notices how closely science and industry are related to military interests and agendas. According the National Science Foundation, in 2002 over half of the federal government's $99 billion research and development budget was spent on national defense (Research on natural resources and the environment got just over 2 percent, space research and technology received over 9 percent, and health-related research received about 24 percent.). When war is serious business, it is profitable to pursue scientific projects that receive military funding. The development of nearly any form of military technology or intelligence can be justified or promoted, no matter how evil, expensive, or ineffective it may be. When the production of war is the heart of an economy, it is war that feeds progress, so progress moves in the direction of war.

Do you want to be a war innovator, or an innovator of something else?

12.

We must figure out a better way of doing things. Now.

Ethics, Earth, and the Secular Sacred

S ince the beginning of reflection, we have tried to make sense of our strange place in the world—a world of nature and our own creations. We form categories, we evaluate. We draw conclusions about the significance of things and revise our ideas, and the process is sometimes quite conscious. We know we are after something, so we ponder and discuss, weighing options and following lines of evidence unto a claim or two that we seem to know for certain. In making sense of the world we make meaning. We construct the world as we know it.

When the Anasazi living in the southwest region of North America a thousand years ago built dwellings and places of worship, they aligned their architecture with the cyclical movements of the sun and moon. In so doing, they responded to their world, marking patterns, noticing and developing theories about what was relevant, and making decisions about what should be set in stone.

These decisions about what mattered, about what was special, were not arbitrary. They depended on the culture's predilections to interpret things a certain way, and therefore on history. They depended on physical events and interpretive tools, such as dreams, visions, and geometric analyses. And such decisions were made from within a complex system of social norms, such as rules about decision-making and the distribution of labour.

Anasazi ideas about what in the world was important, what demanded attention and interaction, were well-grounded, but they were not *necessary*. That is, it could have been another way. Some cultures contemporaneous with the Anasazi happened to agree that the patterns in the night sky held sacred messages. Members of other tenth-century cultures made vastly different decisions about what they took to be sacred, and arrived at different conclusions about what in the world demanded special attention.

Human decisions about what is special about the world depend on rather inflexible facts about the sort of animal we are. It takes a certain kind of visual equipment, and a certain brain, to even be able to see and ponder stars in the night sky. As almost any fifth-grader can tell you, opposable thumbs are necessary for most of the basic physical movements that allow us to fashion objects from matter. On preconscious levels, our bodies pick out what is relevant about our experiences of the world before we have the opportunity to think or decide anything. Conceptions of sacredness are neither arbitrary nor absolute. They are built from the material world and human idiosyncrasies, including what we can know, where we come from, and what we believe.

If we look at the etymology of the word *sacred*, we find a concept with deep references to actions and decisions—to the fact that sacredness is something created. The word *sacred* has ancient origins in the language of what we currently know as Turkey and Syria, and the Latin root of sacred, *sacre*, means "to consecrate." To consecrate is "to set apart, make or declare something to be holy." *Holy* is derived from an Old English term meaning "sound, happy or whole, unimpaired or inviolate." To make something sacred is to confer protected status, and to declare that something should remain sound.

Something created is not absolute, and consecrations can only be made visible by earthly beings. So even with its common references to otherworldliness, the concept of sacredness refers to human actions and responses to the world. The sense that taking something to be sacred involves making it sacred is not a modern insight.

But what does it mean to take something to be sacred?

When we hold something sacred, we hold it in esteem and appreciate it. We do what we can to promote its persistence in the world. Considering things sacred usually implies they should not be damaged or destroyed, so many conceptions of sacredness include principles against defilement or desecration. Then again, sometimes we are supposed to use or transform sacred things in particular ways. Many religions rely on the sense that "sacrifice" means "to make sacred" when they require or extol the occasional sacrifice of whatever is most treasured—even the body of a god.

Religious Sacredness

As a Catholic child I was taught that the priest was able to change bread and wine into the body and blood of Christ, and that the process involved a metaphysical change: that the wafers and wine actually became something else—something sacred, holy and special—through the consecration of the Mass. At the time I was unable to really imagine what it could mean for bread and wine to be part of a human body, or to be part of a god's body, or part of a body that was last seen on the planet around two thousand years ago. And at some level I'm sure I found the idea of eating human flesh to be rather unnerving, if not downright disgusting. In so many ways, accepting the conception of sacredness shared by my family and our church required a suspension of other things I believed.

Still, I understood what it meant for that bread and wine to be sacred. It meant that they had unusual significance. They were otherworldly—somehow connected to beings and forces I could never see. Because they had been consecrated by a priest, they should be treated with respect (they could be reverently consumed, for example, but not dropped on the floor). I knew that interacting with those things had special meaning, and serious consequences.

Now, because I do not subscribe to any religion, I find discussions of sacredness to be dangerous territory. In many common uses of the word, sacredness implies metaphysical beliefs that cannot be proven. It is always important to ask whether a particular conception of sacredness can be rationally defended, and it is equally relevant to ask whether it conforms to intuitions about what is valuable in some deep or special sense.

Dissonances between institutional norms and intuitions are not decisive, but they can be good starting places for critical, open-minded inquiry.

Every religion has a conception of sacredness. When Hindus anoint themselves with ashes, when Jews kiss the Torah, when followers of Shinto tend their household gardens, they enact beliefs about what is sacred, what it means to hold something sacred. These views often depend on strict systems of rules and taboos that aim to keep whatever is sacred shrouded in clouds of mystery and protection. But from within any religious conceptions of sacredness it is possible to notice that other people have different ideas about what is sacred and what sacredness entails.

In a 1970s suburban American culture that was mostly white, the diversity to which I was commonly exposed as a child was religious diversity. I went to Catholic schools and spent time mostly with other Catholic kids, but I lived in a neighborhood that included Protestants and Jews. There were Protestants and Jews in my family, too, and my education in Catholic school included learning about other "great" religions. I was fascinated to learn that Jains were vegetarians, and Muslims bowed each day to Mecca. I knew that my beliefs were not universal, that most people did not believe that bread and wine could be turned into the body and blood of Jesus. Because I knew there were other reasonable options, it was clear that on some level my conception of sacredness involved choice.

There are infinite numbers of ways to interpret the world and our places within it. Accepting a notion of sacredness leads to experiencing a world that is sacred in a particular way. When I was Catholic, I believed in the appropriate pantheon of metaphysical beings, and I interpreted the world in ways that were consistent with the religion in which I'd been raised. That is, I noticed things in the world that confirmed the Roman Catholic conception of what is and is not sacred. I experienced a world that was enchanted by a benevolent force and evaluated by an omnipotent governor. I felt that I was always watched and never alone. I felt safe and good when I was communing with God.

One thing that is so interesting about religious experience is that even when it is founded mostly on indoctrination or irrational belief, it provides a sense of the world that becomes real, that propagates itself in material existence. As systems of beliefs and as institutions, religions themselves are propagated through sacredness. Conceptions of sacredness tie together people of faith in a common set of practices and provide common ways of putting meaning on the world. Sacredness provides a way to *be* in a confusing and contradictory world. Sacredness puts a special aura around things, and so it helps keep those things safe and secure (recall the association of *holiness* with *wholeness*). Some believe sacredness directs them to right behavior and shows the way to salvation or enlightenment. Interestingly, even for nonbelievers, sacredness calls on respect, which is one reason we tend to respect others peoples' views about sacredness. Unless we really do not care about the people in question, or the consequences (too often, probably), we try to avoid harming something someone else thinks of as sacred.

Sacredness creates a rubric for caretaking and a fundamental sense of moral order. In a world where violence is always possible, the absence of sacredness is a scary thing indeed. Perhaps one of the attractions of religion is its ability to provide moral structure and a spiritual haven of safety.

In a world where so much violence and hatred are fed by disagreements over what is sacred, we need to remember the sacred things we can all relate to, and the ways sacredness can bring us together despite the divisions of religious creed.

Secular Sacredness

When religious institutions or specially designated religious people seem the only route to sacred things and resonant communities, religion seems to have cornered the market on sacredness. When religious views imply that sacredness is a purely metaphysical designation, they deny the extent to which *we* consecrate the world and decide what is sacred, and the extent to which sacredness can be a completely earthly concept.

Ideas about sacredness need not be religious. Sacredness is also a cultural concept, especially for those who are not religious, and for religious people with secular values. In the absence of one religion whose beliefs hold us together, in secular societies we hope to aim toward broadly conceived conceptions of the general good, for the group as a whole and for the sub-groups and individuals who make it up. Any good culture, any real democracy, is driven at its core by values that serve the basic interests of the people and groups that comprise it. It is crucial for such societies to articulate thoughtful, life-affirming conceptions of sacredness not attached to a particular religion, or to particular metaphysical beliefs.

Sacredness is a special sort of value. Part of the beauty of democratic values, such as beliefs in fundamental freedoms, is that they constitute a secular conception of sacredness consistent with many different religious and philosophical views. All across the world there is growing consensus that basic human rights are sacred. Differences of religion and culture fade in consequence when we agree about what should be promoted and respected in common cultures, so long as we have the freedom to express and live out our own visions as well.

Secular notions of sacredness are both pragmatic and aesthetic. They are ideas about what matters and what we deem worthy of special respect, and so they can generate ideals. When we are asked to defend secular conceptions of sacredness, we do not provide theistic claims. Instead, we respond by discussing our values, telling stories about why we think something is so special, and describing how it is connected to other things we value. Respect for sacred things can be more like an attitude or a form of attention than a set of rules and principles. We know that conceptions of sacredness are not universal, and that it is useless to try to impose a conception of sacredness on someone who does not agree. We still might want to try to turn people on to what we value, and we might enjoy hearing their views as well. Democracy attempts to create as much space as possible for different ideas about sacredness to coexist.

Holding something sacred in a secular sense means taking it to be sacred for deeply pragmatic reasons. It is to declare certain things sacred because they are adored, or because they are necessary for our own good, or for the flourishing of what we love. To create secular sacredness is to decide that the specialness of the world lies not, or not merely, in metaphysical mystery, but in the mundane wonders found in the live physical world, and even in the things we have in common with people everywhere. To have a secular view of sacredness is to find the sublime in our own experiences and in the world around us.

A conception of sacredness is a reflective, embodied aesthetic that helps ground moral sentiment and judgement. Sacredness helps us feel we live in a world that is special. It gives people reasons to mourn and celebrate, to create and express, to rant and rave and sometimes to ravage. Given how deeply moved people are by feelings and ideas about sacredness—so moved to protect but also to destroy—reflection, critical thinking, and democratic conversation about those values are crucial.

Some traditions would warn that the pragmatic reasons I am discussing here—values that emerge from humans, in our interactions with the material world—cannot ground sacredness, because sacredness is simply a matter of what is blessed or designated by a god. A myth of religion is that sacredness is a given, and that the rules of sacredness should be followed because a not-of-the-world intelligence ordained it to be so. In this conception, sacredness usually involves a fear of punishment or retribution. Such an absolute view demands unquestioning obedience, and so conflicts between religious views and embodied experience must be resolved by the rejection or denial of experience.

In these reflections on sacredness, I do not mean to imply that aspects of our worlds and our lives are sacred for mysterious metaphysical reasons. We can make the world sacred. We can consecrate it.

Creating and responding to the sacredness in the world is not confronting a given. It is engaging a world full of dynamic charm. To have a secular view of sacredness is to look to that world, to experience and knowledge (not superstition or tradition), to tell us what deserves glory.

Earth Is Sacred

It seems almost nonsense to say earth is sacred, because the phrase is a cliché, and because it states something as obvious as the value of life itself. If anything in the real world is sacred, if it makes sense to believe that some things are worthy of special respect, those things depend for their existence on Earth. Visible, yielding, non-negotiable, Earth gave birth to science, to our methods and desire to know. If knowledge requires faithfulness to what we experience in the physical world, then Earth is the basis for all knowing.

As physical beings, we are always dependent on Earth. A delicious bowl of food, a sparkling glass of sweet juice, the oxygen-rich air you are breathing right now: all courtesy of Earth. The comfort of something solid beneath us. Terra firma. All shelter is earthly and Earth cradles every dream.

Earth provides our perspective, yet Earth is too complex, too big to imagine.

Our ground note. The Whole She-Bang.

Earth is our only certain hope.

When we feel bombarded by information about Earth, by documentaries and news reports, by facts about a planet of amazing animals and manmade disasters, it seems easy to forget how close the world is, how absolutely connected we are to earth. Few of us really know the details of our nexus with earth—where the water in the sink flows from, who grew and processed our food, what happens to the garbage after it's taken away on Thursday. We know we are citizens of Earth, but most of us think of our dealings with earth on a much smaller scale. We identify earth in encounters with nature, in the out-of-doors—where we appear to be surrounded by the natural world, where it has been allowed to do its thing without too much interference from difficult humans and our dirty machines.

Our connection to earth is elemental and aesthetic. Don't even your most not-into-nature friends like to sit outside and drink a vodka & tonic on a beautiful summer evening? Fresh air and starshine, green growing life and the critters in our midst. Earth fixes bad moods, and reminds us we are alive. Even among people who seem hellbent on wrecking the planet, it is easy to see how much we adore earth.

> *You stop and gaze at a tall pine tree. You have probably seen a zillion pine trees in your life, even your den is paneled in pine, and every December you sacrifice a pine to celebrate the Christ child, or winter. Today as you look up at this pine tree—you don't even know the name of the tree, for all you know it could be a ponderosa or a spruce—you notice beautiful bright pink*

flowers (or are they cones?) at the top of the tree, far beyond your reach.
What are those pink things? Have they always been there? Aren't they
lovely? There is no one to ask, there is no way to know, but the birds fly back
and forth, from this tree to another. They are singing and busy, and they all
look alike. You focus on one for a while until it flies away faster than your
eyes can follow. Just look at the color of that sky! Those gorgeous pink flower
shapes against that sky. You look and absorb, allowing the vision to linger,
while insects are chirping and stones slide to resting beneath you.

We say our minds become clearer in nature. We say time in nature
provides distance from our lives, and isn't this a strange thing to notice? In
fact, we feel quite alive in the company of the wild. The more-than-human
world distracts and surprises, inviting the fantastically human experience
of amazement. The color of emerald, the scent of red desert, designs on
the back of a bug. Creator or none, we are humbled in the face of something so phenomenal, so complex, so much greater than us. Yet nature lets
us know we are special. Our own earthly transformations are wonders in
themselves. And we are the natural beings who can ponder and discuss
what it means to be good earthly citizens.

Earth is the element: material, solidity, stuff, from flesh to stone to trees
to molten lava. Earth is a place, but earth is also our substance. Earth constitutes and affects us chemically—each breath, bite, and sip takes in earth.
The physical world—not just the intangible matter of psychology—makes
meaning in our worlds. Primary human concepts emerged in relation to
earth and the earthly. The designation of food, the mapping of space,
requirements for survival. Beauty: our love of earth's presentation, our
recognition of scent and color. A sunset, earth moving, atmospheric
vapours refracting in fullblown color. Justice: fair relationships in the face of
the challenges and particularities of life on earth. Having enough, being safe.

Like many other animals, humans thrive by developing practices that keep
the earth a little bit at bay. Cleanliness is among the most basic ways we care for
ourselves, and cleanliness requires a never-ending commitment to remove
earth from our bodies and dwellings. The scent of rich earth in the garden
becomes mud that we wipe from our feet. Earth gets in the way, demands

labor, is something to manage. The dirt, the soil, the mantle of life. Earth is dirty, and as the stuff of all life, it includes the grotesque: nasty smells, bloody gore, rotting debris, slime. Everything we do not want to be. Sometimes it's easy to see what bodyhaters mean when they refer to the earthly as filth.

Loving earth requires loving what we fear, even what we detest. But everything we love, everything we need, presents a gauntlet of contradictions. The complexities of our relationships with earth do not imply that we must treat earth like an enemy instead of a friend. Life's physical realities show us how important, how inescapably necessary it is to exist in cooperation with earth.

It is not too late to make good on our love of Earth, on our sense that it is sacred.

Common Ground

In 1787, the United States of America was the first country to include in its constitution a fundamental separation of church and state. The first amendment articulated a model for the world—a principle that acknowledges the absolute importance of the freedom to believe whatever one chooses, and to enact whatever conception of sacredness truly moves one, as long as others' freedoms are not infringed upon in the process. Yet the conquest of the Americas was fueled by colonialists' overwhelming disregard for the sacredness of the lives of indigenous people, and the desecration of the world that native people held to be sacred. It is a tragic irony that a nation that represents religious freedom was founded on a fundamental inability to recognize the legitimacy of Native American conceptions of sacredness. The bitter truth is that when we bow down to greed and violence, when we value profit above all else, we are not very respectful of sacredness in a form that promotes widespread flourishing.

The secular conception of sacredness I am drawn to has some things in common with the spiritualities of many indigenous cultures. While indigenous belief systems are dynamic and multifaceted, and there are at least as many indigenous religions as there have been native communities on this planet, many share foundational regard for the natural world as a source of knowledge and power. Given the realities of colonialism and neo-colonialism, I am always a bit suspicious when middle class white people go on about their admiration for indigenous ways and thought. But am I a cultural imperialist if I believe aboriginal people got quite a lot right in their conceptions of the cosmos, and what it means to live responsibly on earth?

Simply loving the same earth provides important connections with people of all kinds who believe the world around us, and the beings who inhabit it, are special and worthy of respect. Native Americans refer to *all my relations*, evoking the idea of kinship to name the fact that every person is related to everything in her midst—that our well-being is intrinsically linked to the existence of (all!) others—that on some level we can love all things as we love our kin. Indigenous spiritualities tend to value the ways we are fundamentally tied to all aspects of the world around us, but also to value humans in a special, unique way. Typically, the specialness of human-ity is itself characterized as relational, embodied, and distinguished by its sense of care for others, human and nonhuman alike. Living right, being thankful, and being responsible enough to get the necessary work done are closely related to living well. Engagement with the natural and spiritual worlds through ritual practices, and through appropriate behavior within the community, helps bring prosperity and happiness. Right living requires following some basic rules: Tell your stories. Care for the people and the more than human world. Give thanks. Mourn and celebrate. Dance. Don't take yourself too seriously. Remember the future and the past.

Are even these guidelines too much? Is it possible to have sacredness without paralyzing rules and piety? Notions of sacredness can helpfully direct attention, but is it possible to cultivate such attitudes without also cultivating new dogmas? The concept of sacredness seems so weighty and gilded, a healthy secular skepticism encourages responses to sacredness that are more open than we generally take religious recognition to be.

Kant believed that when something has special value, which he referred to as dignity, we should treat it as an end in itself. Though we might use beings and things that possess dignity, we should not regard them as *mere* means to our own ends. This view provides an interesting model of what it means to regard things that are useful with respect. If sacred things have a kind of dignity, or special significance, then perhaps we should interact with them not like things connected to a god, but instead like the other earthly beings and things we love. We should treat them well, and with respect. We should not deny the depth of our connection to them. It perhaps is obvious that we should not abuse them, but it seems equally true that we should appreciate their presence. That is, we should *enjoy* them.

Cultivating an attitude is tricky moral business. Thoughtfulness or mindfulness (for embodied minds, as much a physical practice as an intellectual one) is a way of directing attention to our connections and the larger world, and away from the seemingly isolated ego. Meditation or even prayer can be practiced without a deity—it is a form of reflection that animates appreciation and respect. Mindfulness assumes an honest orientation, and reminds us of our values. Engaging the world mindfully can be a way of *loving* what you love.

Remarks on Science

Stevie Wonder wrote "when you believe in things that you don't understand, then you suffer," and what philosopher would disagree? An argument for a secular conception of sacredness is an argument against superstition, although it can also encourage dwelling in the beauty of mystery and the universal experience of wonder. On a very basic level we must believe in things we don't really understand—understanding provides only so much guidance in a world too vast, too complex to ever fully know. Even science can help us dwell in wondrous appreciation. Science can be a form of interaction with the world that brings us closer to what we hold sacred, and helps us gain the knowledge we need to protect what we love.

Religion cashes in on the mysteries of life and encourages us to think of too much questioning as insubordination. Secular conceptions of sacredness stand on firmer scientific ground. Although we will never fully understand the world, and its mysteries often inspire inarticulate awe, a sense of sacredness does not require willful ignorance. Scholars don't like to discuss it, but there is an intimate relationship between passion and knowledge. What is passion, what is love, but an appreciation for the specialness of something in the real world? Science is at its best not when it functions like a religion that cannot be questioned, but when it helps us to better know what is most important to us, and when it provides information and tools to help make real the worlds we desire. Science illuminates when it emerges from appreciation and curiosity. We should not assume that scientific scrutiny can only lead to sterile disenchantment.

Think of how we know the weather—inescapable, omnipresent, and profoundly influential on human life. Every culture has a method of understanding and predicting weather, and keeping beings and things safe when weather is harsh. We might see the weather as a creation of an otherworldly force, as a message from the gods or as a form of reward or retribution. But science dispels this view, using sophisticated instruments, advanced methods of record-keeping, and global communication systems to help us know weather as a series of physical events, rather than a cycle of divine dramas. The more we know about planetary cycles, air currents, pollution, and pressure systems, the less likely we are to think of bad weather as an otherworldly force, or divine retribution.

Does scientific knowledge necessarily make us lose touch with the ways our own lives are connected to the climactic cycles in which we are immersed? The forms of understanding that are pursued by science can help us appreciate the weather on its own earthly terms, and can help us understand the details of our relationships with our environments. Storm clouds need not lose their symbolic significance, their poetic effect on the psyche, when we know their physical causes. Science can bring us closer to the details, closer to the matter at hand, which might remain an endless source of wonder or frustration.

Like Anasazi architecture, science is a discourse that detects patterns in the relationships between human actions and well-being. It is science, of course, that makes evident not only what weather is, not only how it affects us, but also how we affect weather and our environments. The more intelligent we become, the more we are able to know about our impact on the world around us, the better equipped we are to figure out how to reduce the harms we cause. When science illuminates, when it allows intimacy with the objects of our respectful curiosity, it creates knowledge that can help us to navigate a complex, dynamic world without harming it. Knowledge can be put to the service of life.

People generally report that they feel good about spending public funds on research that will lead to advancements in science or medicine, but it is not easy to agree on what counts as advancement. Like all other products of history, progress is like an open-ended road trip: even if you don't know where you'll end up, decisions you make along the way determine the next series of options that will be available. It is unfortunate that ideas about what counts as advancement are far more influenced by economic and political factors than by substantive public discussions about what knowledge we need to truly flourish.

Any science is born from a need or desire to know, and every scientific exploration implies decisions about which questions are worth pursuing. But there are crucial differences between science that aims to carry out fundamental beliefs about what is worth preserving and protecting in the world, and science that is motivated by profit alone—somewhat like the difference between science whose goal to understand weather, and science that seeks to control it. If we took the world to be sacred, science and knowledge production in general would be guided by goals of human and planetary well-being. Secular conceptions of sacredness recommend paying attention to the choices that are made in our names, with our resources. Such critical attention requires reliable information and spaces for public discussion and reflection.

One provocative claim of the postmodern turn is the belief that everything, including science, is a myth. The negative interpretation of this view is that no method of science or knowledge-seeking is superior to others, and that there is nothing we can truly know. There is also a more positive interpretation, which is that if all forms of knowledge are contingent human creations—much like stories—then we need to know the purpose of a theory or knowledge-seeking project in order to evaluate its adequacy. Stories are ways of making sense of the world and our place in it, and stories help justify certain ways of being human over others. It is therefore always important to discuss and assess them. But if we have the power to claim or create our own stories, our own myths, the first question is obvious: what stories do we want to create, to propagate?

Critical Theory and the Science of Complexity

Theorizing is a form of knowledge-making that creates order, reifies and challenges power, and informs particular practical decisions and interactions. All sorts of thinkers formulate theories, but academics have raised theorizing to a high art. Although all theorizing addresses abstractions, relationships, and generalities, and theory is a primary form of investigation in mathematics, philosophy, physics, literary criticism, music, and nearly every other discipline, theories about theory tend to stay fairly local. For example, when I recently asked a promising young philosopher of science what he thought about the similarities between scientific theories and political theories, he let me know he found the question inane. He assumed that scientific theories have nothing at all to do with theorizing in softer disciplines, especially those concerned with the interested matter of politics. But he was wrong. Reflection on theory is an important meeting point for science and philosophy, and for academic projects and broader politics.

This essay looks at some connections between different forms of theorizing. Drawing on metaphors developed by theoretical physicists,

41

I consider the usefulness of understanding critical theories such as feminism and postcolonialism as *theories of complexity*, rather than *theories of oppression*.[1]

When we consider critical theories to be primarily about oppression and its legacies, there is a tendency to downplay or overlook their contributions to fundamental philosophical and political discussions regarding the nature of reality, history, knowledge, and ethics. We also give the impression that the project of critical theory is to unearth simple truths that can be stated succinctly and proven directly, in the form of a universally true theory, even though it is clear that the work of critical theory is to explore multifaceted, shifting, and complicated realities. My hunch is that the tendency toward simplicity is fed by loyalty to the outdated methodologies of Marx and Freud, and to a scientific view that identifies truth and knowledge with simple linear facts. Such science is not comfortable with complexity. It aims to reduce complex realities to simple equations, and declares knowledge or success when simple truths are proven.

Contemporary scientific studies of complexity provide a different model for theory-making, and a metaphor that may better serve the projects and concerns of critical theory. Scientists working in theoreti-

---

1. I do not take critical theory to refer exclusively to projects related to Frankfurt School thought. Rather, I use the term to refer to social theories concerned with multiple systems of social power. In addition to versions of feminism concerned with the intersections of sex, race, and class, other examples of critical theory include critical race theories, which engage questions about race and racism in relation to complex historical analyses of law, economy, and sexual difference, and postcolonial perspectives, which take theory to require explorations of the complex interweavings of state power, culture, race, gender, and land. Critical theory also includes social ecologies that focus on the ways harm to the natural world is felt most directly by those who lack economic power, and those who are symbolically linked to nature in demeaning ways. Critical theorists agree that forms of life and systems of exploitation are webs of connections, and that any adequate critical or liberatory discourse must know and respond to these connections. Of course, that leaves open many potential areas of disagreement.

cal physics and the interdisciplinary sciences find that simple physical laws produce a world that is infinitely complex, consisting of elaborate components, such as beings, things, systems, and networks, that are deeply relational. This view calls for projects that explore the relationships between simple truths and complex realities, and require methods that are multidisciplinary, open-ended, and pluralist.

Here I will discuss some of the differences between simple and complex things and theories, and illustrate the usefulness of the scientific metaphor of complexity for critical social theories. In turn, I show that critical theory offers science a more thorough conception of interdisciplinarity, and a challenging model of political academic engagement.

The Simple and the Complex

Something that is "simple" can be fully conveyed with a brief explanation, but something that is "complex" calls for much more. In the words of a mathematician, the complexity of an object "is directly proportional to the length of the shortest possible description of that object" (Casti, 9). Simple entities, such as crystals, and simple relations, such as ionic exchanges, can be captured in simple equations and definitions. But to adequately describe complex things like ecosystems, economies, and human lives, we need lengthier descriptions. For example, if I open up a 500-page book and find that its text consists of nothing but the sentence "All work and no play make Wendy an unhappy girl," printed over and over again, I can turn around and describe the book to you, quite completely, in one sentence. But if I want to describe a complex work like Toni Morrison's *Beloved* to you, many more sentences would be required to fully convey the thing. It is even arguable that the "best description" of a work of great literature would be provided by reading to you every word of the book, because the interrelatedness of particular words and groups of words to each other and the whole text are so crucial. Perhaps not even that would be enough.

In this deceptively simple definition of complexity, we can see that what seems to be simple is likely not so simple. Many issues concerning language, interpretation, context, and purpose determine what qualifies as a "best description" of anything, and so determinations of complexity and simplicity are always somewhat relative to the project or audience at hand. If you are not taken with literature, you might be content with a Cliff Notes description of a Toni Morrison novel. If you are not familiar with a particular symbolic system, or its abstract concepts of reference, a simple linear equation such as $E=mc^2$ might not serve as a good description of anything.

Claims about simplicity and complexity are not merely about explanations of things. They are facts about matter itself. Contemporary scientific studies of complexity emerged from quantum mechanics, the theoretical arm of experimental physics. In quantum mechanics, scientists find the formulas that predict the probabilities of possible outcomes of experiments, and use their findings to describe the framework into which all physical theory must fit. Known as the discourse of quarks and superconductors, quantum mechanics pursues bottom-line truths about the world, such as the simple truth that elementary energetic "particles" follow rather predictable, universal, and immutable laws. But physics cannot stop there, with what is explainable in simple terms, because those simple elements form "complex adaptive systems"—beings and systems that can learn and respond, and that are not predictable.

In his book *The Quark and the Jaguar: Adventures in the Simple and the Complex*, physicist Murray Gell-Mann provides a representative list of complex adaptive systems:

> . . . a human child learning his or her native language, a strain of bacteria becoming resistant to an antibiotic, the scientific community testing out new theories, an artist getting a creative idea, a society developing new customs or adopting a new set of superstitions, a computer programmed to evolve new strategies for winning at chess, and the human race evolving ways of living in greater harmony with itself and with the other organisms that share the planet Earth (9).

A distinguishing feature of complex adaptive systems is their ability to effect change in relation to information about patterns in the world. Here is Gell-Mann's description of what it means for a complex adaptive system to learn:

> A complex adaptive system acquires information about its environment and its own interaction with that environment, identifying regularities in that information, condensing those regularities into a kind of "schema" or model, and acting in the real world on the basis of that schema. In each case, there are various competing schemata, and the results of the action in the real world feed back to influence the competition among those schemata (17).

Theorizing is one way complex human systems (socially-embedded individuals and groups) develop and test the schemata through which we know the world. We can accurately describe initiating conditions, fundamental elements, and basic systems with simple explanations and equations. There are neat physical laws from which everything emerges, and to which all objects are subject. But these laws include the existence of unpredictable behaviors and events, labyrinthine relations of communication and interdependence, accumulated and ongoing historical effects, and also chance and chaos. The result is a physical universe of intricate, overlapping worlds—a nexus of complex living and nonliving systems that cannot be described in the simple laws and linear equations that fully capture the initiating conditions. These systems are adaptive and dynamic, and they are transformed in relation with each other. Clearly, such a world is best understood through approaches that are themselves multifaceted, multi-leveled, and multidisciplinary.

Theories of complexity in the sciences are driven by the recognition that the living world cannot be adequately described through simple equations, because it is a world of complex adaptive systems that are dynamic, because they interact and "learn." Exploring complexity requires abandoning the illusion that all good science is atomizing, breaking things down into simple constituent elements. Elaborate and interwoven systems of persistence, interaction, and response are not simple decipherable objects. Theories of complexity in physics resonate with work in evolutionary biology and ecological sciences, which are also deeply historical and relationship-sensitive, and which take ontological borders to be interesting precisely because they are permeable and difficult to decipher.

Philosopher Mary Midgley describes the investigative methods demanded by complexity through the metaphor of a mountain. To learn about a mountain one cannot rely exclusively on information gotten from looking through a microscope or telescope, or on what is evident when one observes food chain relationships or seismic shifts. Knowing a mountain requires all of these inquiries and many more, and it requires studying the mountain from many different perspectives. Study or theorizing about complex beings and systems—things as "vast, complex, and relatively distant" as mountains—requires information obtained from many different perspectives and different methods, and so also requires methods for evaluating, translating, and conjoining different sorts of information. It also calls for open-endedness, because complex systems are dynamic. Over time there will always be new things to learn about the mountain, its many constituent components, and their complex webs of relation.

Critical Theory

What might all this have to do with feminism, postcolonial theory, and other critical approaches beyond the sciences? As in the physical sciences, part of the work of critical theorists is to analyze how simply-statable truths ("systems of race and gender enable exploitation") play out in complex ways, in complex contexts, and how they are reinforced and resisted through myriad social forms and practices. Critical theories engage social worlds (and sometimes ecosocial worlds) that are infinitely complex. Critical theorists hold that in order to increase understanding and develop effective strategies for positive change, theorizing ought to address multiple strands of causality and meaning, and the relationships among them. Because its questions cover such a wide range of material, and because it sees most objects of inquiry as rather complex phenomena, critical theory requires multiple disciplinary and methodological approaches. At least in theory, the logic of critical theory is inherently pluralist and self-reflexive. It is these features, along with politics, that put the "critical" in critical theory.

Of course, few people would say that complexity is what critical theory brings to the table. Feminism, for example, is described not as a theory of social complexity, but as a set of positions critical of sexism or gender oppression, or celebratory of female perspectives and particularities, or skeptical concerning the necessity of sex and gender as organizing concepts in human reality. But a critical focus on gender (or another identity or form of power) naturally opens out into a deeply complex project. Feminism does assert some version of a relatively simple empirical fact, coupled with a fairly simple ethical claim: social worlds tend to present inadequate options to women, categorically, and the conditions that enable and further that oppression ought to be eliminated or transformed. But what seems to be a simple description of reality is really not so simple. Any respectable feminist theorist knows that considerations of sex and gender must include attention to race, class, sexuality, and more. This is because the meanings and experiences of "woman" are highly contingent, and maintained in complex, dynamic relations with other social and physical forms. No woman is *just* a woman, no man is just a man, and we all embody gender as a locus of other forms of power. Sex and gender do not exist in pure forms in individual bodies, or in the social systems that organize human bodies, because human lives and social systems inevitably include overlapping forms of power and identity, including race, religion, nation, and class. No one can slice off the part of itself that is sex or gender, although sex and gender form the texture of nearly every human life.

As a critical theory, feminism knows gender to be complex—a patterned phenomenon that varies widely over time and space, that exists in as many forms as there are forms of human life, and that is part of complicated and dynamic discursive and physical worlds. The projects of feminist theory are nothing less than describing and probing the categories and practices that maintain forms of identity and forms of human life (including gender, race, clan, and species, economy, nation, and culture), and investigating how these are deeply interwoven with each other and with a complex and endangered physical world.

It is not difficult to establish the fact that critical theories see truths as complex, at least in a minimal sense, because critical theories hold that a good description of reality is interdisciplinary and multi-layered, or "lengthy" in the term favored by physical scientists. Other potential meeting points between critical theory and theories of complexity include rejections of reductionist approaches to knowledge production, and overlapping political interests.

Reductions

Even though simplicity lies in the eyes of the beholder, in factories of knowledge production the appeal of simplicity is fairly universal—it lies in the attractiveness of rock-bottom conclusions that can be presented as linear expressions. Mary Midgely argues that the scientific paradigm that upheld simple empirical truths as the model of true knowledge was historically influential because "it struck people as a more honourable and decent world-view than a grovelling and superstitious terror of the gods" (30).

The problem is not that simple descriptions are not true. It is not necessarily a mistake to pursue simple observable truths. The problem is the fact that influential institutions and cultures christen simple truths *real* knowledge, and vilify less reductive (more complex) methods. A good example of debates between complex and reductionist approaches is found in philosophy, regarding theories of the mind. There is a fairly popular view that sees minds as reducible to chemical processes in the brain, and that considers everything that we know as "consciousness" to be irrelevant in constructing useful and accurate models of the mind.

Such a reductionist project is rejected by theories of human minds that investigate simply-stated truths about brain chemistry in relation to a whole organism, its practices, experiences, and beliefs, and its immersion in particular social and ecological environments. Which sort of theory would provide more accurate and useful ideas about minds? The answer depends on the inquirer's interests and goals. A pharmaceutical company might need nothing more than a chemical description; a teacher needs a much more complex picture of minds.

Discourses of complexity are powerful antidotes to views that reduce incredibly complicated realities to simple truths. Scientific engagements with complexity question methods that aim to reduce all truths to linear equations or rock-bottom simple facts about the world, such as the view that the best science of mind describes chemical processes in the brain. Other reductions, such as the view that to be human is to be rational (only), to live is to be selfish (only), or that organisms and processes are constituted by solid borders and are therefore completely knowable apart from the systems that support them, cannot survive analyses that take seriously a world of difference, chaos, and vastly complicated interrelatedness.

Although complexity theorists in the sciences argue against scientific approaches that aim to reduce complex truths to simple truths, an emphasis on complexity is not meant to be a rejection of simple truths, or the pattern-seeking investigations through which they are constructed. Complexity theorists see the discovery of a simple truth as an invitation to investigate new broad questions, because there is always a wider context into which a new, simply-expressible discovery must be incorporated to become useful knowledge. Fruitful paths of inquiry are forged through curiosity about relationships between simple truths and complex realities. Theories that recognize complexity therefore can include the bottom-line theories to which reductionists cling.

Simplicity should not be the only goal of knowledge, but simplicity is a powerful tool of knowing. We could not notice or understand complex systems if we could not identify and interpret patterns, and descriptions of patterns are simplifications, expressible in simple equations.

When they describe reality well, simple equations capture something that is unifyingly true about the world, like 2+2=4, "Organic beings have basic chemical requirements for health," "Where race or gender are present, oppression is often found," or "A rose is a rose is a rose." Simple equations can capture facts that are as universally true as it is possible to be.

But a simple equation never captures a truth that is the *only* thing we need to know about what it describes. Simple truths always leave remainders, and so knowing a simple truth about something—even a profound simple truth—always leaves us with only part of the story. Statements about the beauty of roses tell us nothing about pollination. Unless you know the mass of the planet you're on, you won't be able to calculate its gravitational force, even if you understand Einstein's theory of general relativity. If you know the chemical composition of a thing, but don't know how it tastes, you cannot make a good judgement about whether it is good food. Knowing one powerful truth about human behavior is most useful when it is considered in relation to many other things. Without such integration, simple truths are blinding rather than illuminating.

Perhaps the strongest argument against reductionist approaches is the incredible complexity of the physical world, and its nexus with human life. Appreciating complexity includes not only stressing the extent to which the world is complicated, but also that the subjects and objects of observance, experience, and study are many-layered, changing, and rather unpredictable. Complexity theories more accurately reflect experience, because they describe reality as more like a Navajo rug, and less like a linear equation. Thinking about complexity is powerful, because it is so deeply resonant, despite the scholastic difficulties of adequately capturing such analyses in equations or words.

Critical Reductions

The theoretical projects of critical social theories are exceedingly complicated. Many of us have become accustomed to hearing phrases referring to "the intersections of race, class, and gender," and we forget just how complex and multidimensional such relational ontologies actually are. Critical theories take the subjects and objects of knowledge to be constituted and transformed through relationships, and they emphasize how physical and social interdependencies affect existence on all layers, from the physical and chemical to the epistemic, to the global economic. Critical theory sees reality as historical, ever-unfolding, and affected by chance and unknowns.

Yet critical theories are often described as theories of oppression, or analyses of how oppression functions. It is true that critical theories trace the relationships among harmful social forms, such as racism, capitalism, and colonialism. Many critical theories assume or assert that there something like a "logic of domination" that informs most human social order, creating and maintaining systems and practices of violence and exploitation on both micro and macro levels. Approaches that are explicitly tied to identity, such as critical race theory and queer theory, often focus on specific histories of oppression and resistance in hostile contexts. Perhaps this is why it is thought that the "critical" in critical theory says it all, and that political critique or identity politics is all that lies at the heart of the project.

Knowledge that the world is complex does not eliminate the tendency to emphasize simple truths, or to gravitate toward reductive explanations. Marx and Freud are omnipresent ghosts inspiring critical attempts to find fundamental, simple truths that will cause the scales to fall from our eyes. Simple truths (capitalism is exploitation; the unconscious is a gateway to knowing the self) are powerful because they capture and unify reality. Theories of oppression attempt to identify hidden lines of power and "root causes" that shape patterns of injustice and harm. Isolating and analyzing particular features or systems of oppression is as crucial to understanding the social world as $E=mc^2$ is to understanding matter. Simple truths can also be politically powerful, when they state truths that are not widely acknowledged. As obvious as it may be to some people that racism and sexism exist, naming the simple truth of the fact of oppression can still be illuminating or disarming in some contexts.

At the same time, like all theories, theories of oppression are partial. What is most interesting to theories of oppression are the particulars of oppression. Theories of oppression that overemphasize simple conclusions, such as the ubiquitous nature of domination, risk reducing complex issues to simple equations. Simplification makes it less likely that we will pay attention to phenomena that don't fit the pattern, such as contexts where domination is absent or effectively mitigated, or contradictions, such as the fact that being dominated can feel exactly like being free. Recall how Marx and Freud's own commitments to simple and one-dimensional explanations prevented them from appreciating the complicating data that stood right before their eyes (such as race for Marx, and sexual violence for Freud). It is not just the thread of continuity and resemblance that make phenomena interesting and relevant to theorizing. Counterevidence is key to the growth of any discourse.

Fortunately, the combination of pluralist methodologies and political commitments is useful for keeping reductive tendencies in check. The primary impetus for feminist theorizing of "intersections" came from political demands for feminism that was appropriately attentive to a far wider range of lives and experiences, and especially to race, sexuality, disability, and class. The challenge put forth in real political contexts was met in works such as Gloria Anzaldúa's *Borderlands/La Frontera*, which articulated feminism that was fundamentally committed to addressing multiple complex realties—both the facts of oppression, and the complicating contradictions that render any simple description or explanation inadequate. Anzaldúa's work is an excellent example of theory that offers a range of constructive insights regarding identity, culture, and their enmeshments with/in language. Focusing only on Anzaldúa's criticism of sexism, colonialism, and homophobia neglects the substantial positive contributions of her work, such as her theory of intuitive knowledge, or *la facultad*:

> *La facultad is the capacity to see in surface phenomena the meaning of deeper realities, to see the deep structure below the surface. It is an instant "sensing," a quick perception arrived at without conscious reasoning. It is an acute awareness mediated by the part of the psyche that does not speak, that communicates in images and symbols. . . . The one possessing this sensitivity is excruciatingly alive to the world (38).*

Critical theory aims not only to understand oppressive social systems and patterns, but also to change them, and to encourage alternatives. Behind any evaluative critique lies some positive vision, and methods for locating and developing alternative paradigms and possibilities. For example, critical race theorists show how the deep social significance of racial difference and injustice cannot be adequately addressed by existing civil rights legislation. In criticizing influential legal trends, they offer analyses of how oppression is fueled even by laws that aim to eradicate injustice. This analysis could not be offered without underlying conceptions of what a more just system requires, and how different ways of understanding and interacting with racial realities could produce better results. Critical race theories include or assume views about history, the significance of law, effective political strategies, and the relationships among various spheres of meaning. It is not inaccurate to characterize this work as theorizing about oppression or racism (proving a root truth such as "civil rights law tends to support, rather than subvert, existing race relations"), but it is important to also draw attention to the deeper implications of the work, and to question the view that its relevance is limited to concerns about oppression or even race.

Politics

I have been discussing theorizing as though it is a distinct practice and an isolated category of knowledge production. That image is a fiction, of course. Theory is practice, and it informs and is shaped by myriad other practices, material conditions, and political realities. I've characterized theory as the effort to understand and describe "reality," but theory is no distanced knower, gazing upon reality from above and attempting a perfect sketch. As a form of interactive reflection, theory does aim to capture and convey, but those aims are never pure, disinterested, or only intellectual.

It is perhaps easy to appreciate complexity in abstraction, and even to see it all around us. But how do complex theories move in the world? Like any science, the science of complexity aims to predict outcomes. In the laboratory, complexity theorists develop computer simulators that incorporate complex arrays of factors. Scientists interested in complexity have developed a computer model that simulates the conditions in Earth's primordial soup, so as to figure out how matter originally self-organized into living cells, and software programs that simulate the dynamics of the stock market, so as to detect hidden and emergent patterns in the "econosphere." In science, the successes of complexity theory are measured in the predictive power of such models.

The successes of critical theory are measured differently. Its conclusions are considered useful insofar as they predict in a much looser sense. They may provide general rubrics of understanding that are most directly useful because they explain or help us negotiate reality. More importantly, critical theory aims to *direct* through its predictions, and it does so without apology or denial. Anzaldúa's agenda is to validate and encourage *la facultad* as legitimate knowledge. Informed by the experience of those who have been marginalized by existing legal systems, critical race theorists recommend specific alternative approaches. Critical theory does not pretend its political agendas can be extracted from epistemic goals.

One of the recent great successes of critical theory has been the emergence of a complex and multifaceted movement for global justice, often characterized as the "anti-globalization" movement. The hallmark of this movement is its multiplicity—it attempts to incorporate a range of concerns, from environmental issues to international human rights, from social justice (race, sex, sexuality) to the workings of global capital, from indigenous land rights to the demands of local workers. Incorporating a key critical theory insight about the connectedness of various systems and realities, the movement for global justice asserts complex analyses of oppression, and complex understandings of what is necessary for planetary flourishing. Ecofeminism, a significant thread in the movement for global justice, is an example of a perspective that begins with attention to the relationships between exploitative social relations and human disregard for the natural world. Such politics can confound, because they cannot be captured in a sound byte or identified with a singular figure or agenda, and the difficulty of representing and building upon a coalition-based movement can make the counterproductivity of chaos painfully evident. There is no denying that complexity demands careful communication across disparate discourses. But even when activists disagree about particular issues, or when they believe that there is some "root cause" (such as "greed" or "capitalism") driving the various systems they protest, they are committed to a political approach that incorporates attention to a range of overlapping and interwoven agendas. They are committed, one might say, to *politics of complexity*.

Critical theory did not create the movement for global justice. Rather, critical theories generated inside and outside of the academy have articulated the need for multifaceted political approaches, and they continue to provide and inspire activist analyses of the character of the connections among seemingly disparate systems. Regardless of particular outcomes, or the destiny of particular movements (which themselves are never simple things, but clusters of related events, exchanges, and positions), critical theoretical approaches have informed a new form of global political movement.

The primary difference between critical theory and scientific studies of complexity is political. Critical theorists in the humanities, arts, and law are explicitly driven by ethical commitments. The work presents itself as willing to question the political and institutional status quo in the service of knowledge and justice. Critical theory stresses that the world's complexity includes abuses of power that can only be understood through multiple and varying perspectives and approaches. In the academy, interdisciplinarity was at first a political project, meant to further knowledge by including formerly excluded voices and perspectives, but also to transform epistemic and pedagogical endeavors, and to create more democratic institutions.

Not much in the work on complexity in the physical sciences indicates serious interest in engaging complex forms of embodied social power such as race, gender, or capital. Theorizing about complexity in the sciences is critical of disciplinary orthodoxies in the sciences, but it does not address or account for the forms of social power that interest critical theorists. When scientific theories of complexity look at social and political issues, their questions concern statistical outcomes and likelihoods, not deep causes and influences. Most scientific work on complexity is exceedingly well funded by government agencies, corporations, and the military, because of its relevance to business, medicine, and weapons development (representative work on complexity in the sciences can be accessed at the website of the Santa Fe Institute, www.santafe.edu).

Although complexity theorists in the sciences are not identified with the political left, they often describe themselves as motivated by fascination with the amazing physical world, and as dedicated to preserving natural and cultural diversity. But their projects are not aimed at reducing the disparities created by ecological or cultural imperialism. And their interdisciplinary collaborations do not extend very far—while their projects sometimes include economists and quantitative political scientists, complexity theorists in the sciences generally do not tend to seek out collaborations with social theorists, or theorists whose work questions the wisdom of militarism or capitalism.

Nonetheless, there is no epistemic obstacle to projects that incorporate complex understanding of physical reality, social systems, and power. Critical theory and complexity theory both encourage carefully wrought ontologies and excellent communication across disciplines and practices. Politically, critical theorists and complexity theorists share fascination with and regard for the material world, and an interest in promoting planetary flourishing. Perhaps acknowledging the depth of our connection to the fragile world is the first place for innovators who see complexity to engage across differences.

Of course, critical theorists and complexity theorists could also share collaborative projects. Complexity theorists in the sciences like to make models out of data, to test their predictive skills and to help conceptualize possible futures. Working together, critical theorists and complexity theorists could address some interesting questions, like: What kinds of institutions are most likely to effectively promote ethics of caring, rather than greed? What form of economy would allow us to extract the pursuit of knowledge, and even art, from the pursuit of oppressive power?

Justice, Joy, and Feminist Sex

This essay is dedicated to the memory of Linda Weiner Morris,
whose friendship brought me joy.

eminist ethics should promote both justice and joy.
Feminism therefore requires radical critical openness to a
plurality of positions, motivations, commitments, and priorities regarding sex. In feminist philosophy, innovative and fruitful projects might
also result from intercourse across apparently intractable differences.

There is not a chasm between different feminist positions—there
is a canyon filled with interesting life. Even when you share goals with
the gals on the other side, ponderous obstacles encourage inertia. But
if you begin the annoying journey, you'll soon find the rugged land
compelling. At the bottom of the canyon is a sparkling estuary that
empties out into a glorious rough sea.

Feminist Difference and Ethics

In recent years, there seems to have been significant political movement in feminist communities regarding the politics of sexuality. I wish
I could say that recent feminist theorizing was as dynamic and fascinating. Given the institutions in which we work, it is difficult for feminist academics to produce work that seems as alive and engaged as
discussions in other communities sometimes seem to be.

Political practice is the best source of new energy for political the-orizing, so I am interested here in tracing parallels between feminist political controversies about sex and scholarly debates about ethics. Risking hope, I am trying on the view that movement can inspire movement, and that in the context of solidarity a long-term view of even deep disagreement encourages attention to points of connection, and to developmental shifts.

An example of a perennial feminist controversy that may not be as intractable as it appears is a debate about ethics itself. There are long-standing feminist disagreements about rules and norms—about whether there should be any, and whether anyone should have the authority to enforce decisions about right and wrong. One "side" of the debate is a tendency to reject any attempt to articulate norms. This view is expressed as a rejection of rules, moralizing, and judgmentalism on the ground that these are inherently constraining, harmful, or unfair. An anti-norm bias is typically identified with sexual libertarianism, as artic-ulated in the classic book *Powers of Desire: The Politics of Sexuality* (Snitow, Stansell, and Thompson, 1983). But even many feminists who do not identify with libertarianism see themselves as rule-breakers and rene-gades within society, or within feminism—as defenders of personal free-dom in the face of repression, and as thoughtful critics of rules that only protect the interests of those with privilege. Resistance to regressive or confining views about what it means to be a good woman is basic to feminism, and self-reflexive criticism is a hallmark of feminist politics.

But of course any rejection of norms must itself rely on norms, and so the renegade impulse creates an interesting paradox in feminist ethics (I argue below that Drucilla Cornell's conception of "ethical fem-inism" caves under the weight of the paradox). In critically evaluating the real world and recommending alternatives, feminism necessarily asserts ethical values and goals. As political theorizing, feminism ana-lyzes power and evaluates the potential for social change in relation to feminist norms. Feminism therefore cannot avoid normativity. Audre Lorde's famous essay "Uses of the Erotic: The Erotic as Power," which hinges on a distinction between the erotic and the pornographic, and which emphasizes the power of choice and agency, is an influential example of feminism built on the assumption that feminist norms can and should be consciously pursued.

Along with the conflicting views that feminism should reject norms and that feminism should promote good choices, feminism questions the notion that ethics is always a matter of intention, and that political agency is reducible to what is conscious. Psychoanalytic and other semiotic approaches emphasize how political and ethical agency is shaped by factors beyond conscious awareness and control. If ethics is not a purely conscious matter, feminist ethics need not characterize moral and political life as reducible to questions about articulating and following rules and norms. If there are layers of ethical being that are influential in subtle and uncontrollable ways, discussions of norms should be informed by insights regarding those less accessible aspects of moral being, and the wide variety of human political agency. Feminism therefore needs sophisticated theories of moral development and "the unconscious," and values that are pluralist and open-ended.

When common political goals or discourses exist, attention to the subtle layers of ethical life allows us to see beyond the dichotomous conflict between a simplistic rejection of norms, on the one hand, and the moralizing tendencies that have seemed basic to some versions of feminism, on the other. It may also open up the space for some serious cross-pollination among different approaches to feminism, feminist theory, and ethics.

Ethics as Justice and Joy

Keeping in mind various feminist positions, I want to investigate some of the relationships among feminism, ethics, and sex. It will be helpful to first clarify what I mean by ethics, so I offer several nonanalytic foundational claims.

(1) *Somehow, we are ethical beings.* We (who sense ourselves as ethical) care about others and are moved by the interests of others. Caring

is woven thoroughly into our bodies and consciousness and, hence, our values and deliberations. We are fundamentally dependent and social, but we also sense ourselves as isolated and independent. Despite this independence, our commitments to others, and to our projects together, create frameworks in which others' well-being remains central in our conceptions of the good.

(2) *Ethics should promote joy.* Ethical principles, practical wisdom, affective responsiveness, and virtues help us live good lives—lives in which we are able to explore possibilities, seek happiness, joy, and contentment, and coexist in ways that are more like communion and less like war. As ethical beings we move toward relationships and communities characterized by cooperation, honesty, and fulfillment of many different life options, including unique potential for well-being, pleasure, knowledge, and even brilliance. Philosophical ethics pursue understanding of the barriers to ethical life, and also of the ways people value and promote health, integrity, and other aspects of flourishing.

(3) *Ethics should promote justice.* Ethics help us identify, address, and work to reduce harm and injustice. Ethics help us articulate and negotiate personal and communal goals and limits in terms of respect, doing the right thing, and being fair. Values and evaluations can help us find alternatives to ways of being and social structures that are directly or indirectly exclusionary, harmful, or oppressive. Ethics is useful for renouncing the notion that those who are white, male, rich, or straight are inherently more deserving of good lives or the deeply significant freedoms and material resources needed to pursue flourishing. Ethics assist us in naming injustice, and figuring out how to respond in its presence. Because the work of naming injustice is historical as well as immediate, ethics must be somewhat backward-looking.

(4) *Ethics should attend to the psyche.* Ethics must attend to the unconscious aspects of the psyche, because this is where we originally become ethical beings, and social persons with meaningful, particular identities. Any ethical position that takes as its starting point resistance to long-standing injustice and deep harm must be aware that such histories shape identities and embodied minds. Unconscious drives and

motives develop within systems of oppression, and they are not entirely accessible, transparent, or trustworthy. Nor are they necessarily evil. The joyful aspects of life that help stoke ethical being resonate in its unconscious layers. Ethics must attend to the fact that people are complicated and multiplicitous, and should conceive of practices, experiences, and identities as fundamentally complex.

(5) *Ethics should be forward-looking.* Ethical responses within exceedingly oppressive contexts include visions and aspirations toward more liberated forms of being and relating. Commitments to forward-looking ethical projects lead us to engage experiences and desires critically, but also to see them as possible sources of information and inspiration. Ethics help maintain hope.

Ethics should promote both justice and joy, but justice and joy can indicate very different projects—one more normative, the other more exploratory. In practical moral life, we experience tensions between the avoidance of evil and the pursuit of joyful living; between a thirst for justice (the eradication of injustice, oppression, and the influence of corrupting power) and drives toward contentment (the experience of life as fundamentally worthwhile, mutual caretaking of those we love, the ability to partake in the diverse pleasures of existence). A tension between a thirst for justice and a drive toward joy runs parallel to debates between different philosophical approaches to ethics. It is evident between consequentialist and deontological perspectives, between evaluations of actions and evaluations of character, between rules and values, and between justice and care.

Joy is a complex emotion. It is a feeling or experience of deep pleasure, with the higher-order awareness of being profoundly satisfied. We experience joy as contentment, ecstasy, awe, or delight. Joy is deeply physical. We feel joy in response to a world that we love, or in relief from hardships and pain. We find joy in gratitude, and in a sense of well-being. Joy is ethically important because it is more than a feeling—it also sparks and expresses knowledge. It reminds us of what we love and with whom we are bound. It can tell us what to do, and why. Joy can brings us back to a rock-bottom knowledge that life is good or worth-while. One of the most interesting things about joy is how closely it is related to love. Personally, I have never experienced true joy that was not somehow in the company of love.

Ethics requires diligent evaluation and attention to justice, but it also requires the wisdom that comes from dwelling in layers that refuse regulation. Joy, fear, and other fundamentally affective responses inform moral imagination. Emotional and physical responses are even powerful enough to provide the experience of free-dom in the midst of oppression. Ethical theory rarely includes con-sideration of the embodied and affective sources of ethical care and motivation. Though the scholarly field feminist ethics has given an extraordinary amount of attention to caring as a moral response, it has given far less consideration to the moral significance of joy and other affective dimensions of responsiveness (one exception is feminist scholarly attention to maternal love). Perhaps this lack of philosophi-cal interest is due to the fact that joy has been assimilated to happiness, and ethical concern with happiness is easily reduced to traditional lib-eral utilitarian arguments. My discussion of joy is neither a utilitarian argument for happiness as *summum bonum* nor an argument for the unqualified freedom to pursue happiness. Rather, I am interested in joy as something more complex than happiness, as one of many sources of ethical being. For example, many experience the physical connection and ecstasy of sexuality and erotic engagement as sources of self-respect and loving regard for others. Other interesting sources of ethical dispositions include the joy that is sometimes found in rela-tionships of care, the development of moral knowledge, and the feel-ing that accompanies a nonviolent orientation toward others. Joy in these senses is not one-dimensional. It can even depend on experiences of pain and suffering.

Joy is not morality (indeed, often the pursuit of joy involves self-ishness and harm to others), but joy can be deeply relevant to moral life. How might feminists integrate concern with fighting injustice and with the desire to further happiness, flourishing, and joy? What should we do, and how should we be, when justice and joy conflict? These questions are highlighted in feminist thinking about sex.

Sex in Feminism

It is easy to caricature first world feminist sexual politics as the obsessions of people with nothing better to worry about, but the bodily nature of gender, and the inescapable nexus of gendered life, race, class, and sexuality, keeps sex at the heart of nearly any feminism. Although its specific expressions are often shaped by systems of social privilege, feminism's interest in sexuality is necessary. Sexuality is where the gendered personal-and-political are conjoined, where masculine power is nakedly presented. For women and children, it is also a common site of harm. In addition, feminist frenzy concerning sex is a product of the sexiness of exposing what we are ambiguously encouraged to keep under wraps. It is fed by women's desire and need to have more control over sexuality, and to have good sex.

In certain versions of feminism so much seems to hang on sex, as though discovering the truth about sex and its relation to other forms of power will result in a fundamental freedom, and as though the relationships among sexual autonomy, pleasure, and empowerment were seamless. But this view of sex is built on optimistic assumptions about the control anyone can have over her own embodied and social responses. Erotic responses and desires are woven from cultural and personal fantasies about sexual engagement, many of which are shaped to serve masculinist interests. How could moral and political projects that aim to increase and transform women's power *not* be concerned with the intricacies of sex? How could feminist attention to sex not be contentious and heated? Sex has many meanings that depend on exclusions and boundary-marking, all informed by norms of gender. Sexual spaces and interactions are denoted by where we touch, whom we touch, how we talk or think or write or move, and how we feel when we do the things we do. All the particularities about you will determine what you take to be sexual, and what turns on the part of you that gets turned on when you're feeling sexy. Sex refers to a realm of physical intimacy, fantasy, and response: pleasure, orgasms, extraordinary touch and communication. It often refers to genital sensation, making out, nakedness and dress-up. It refers to bodies coming together, in space or in the imagination, and sharing information about desire—about what alights their intense pleasure and excitement.

While sex is usually taken to refer to genital or orgasmic contact, it is not reducible to those, or to anything else we might think sex is. Alongside the fact that sexuality always sits within a nexus of cultural, racial, and class formations, the complexities of personal histories, political positions, and other aspects of identity make it impossible to characterize any one opinion as *the* feminist position on sex. And the differences between feminist positions are not trivial—it was probably inevitable that the libertarian feminist response to sexual repression would confront the conscious rejection of domination head-on in the feminist sex wars of the 1980s and '90s, fought over the ethics of sadomasochism, pornography, prostitution, and sex with men. It is tempting to describe those controversies as between two fundamentally different sets of priorities. In the literature, libertarian positions that aimed to free women from moralism and repression were pitted against the view that feminist consciousness leads to the rejection of all vestiges of oppression and violence against women. At times the debates sounded like contests for the position "most victimized by other feminists." Sex radicals complained that they were repressed by feminism. Other feminists complained that sadomasochists and proponents of pornography accepted patriarchal norms and were therefore agents of patriarchal harm. Put differently, sex radicals were driving toward joy, while other feminists were concerned about justice.

In the libertarian arguments put forth by many sex radicals, there was an assumption that breaking the laws of heteropatriarchy or "correct" feminism was itself a radical departure from oppressive norms. In fact, libertarian positions generally defended freedoms in traditional liberal terms. As Bat-Ami Bar On has argued, the liberal conception of individual agency and social change that lay beneath libertarian positions betrayed their radical intentions—politically, it is not radical to hold experiences and feelings exempt from critical engagement, or to eschew all forms of ethical judgement. More importantly, libertarian feminists generally failed to provide a nuanced articulation of *why* certain freedoms and pleasures matter, and how they are relevant to feminism.

Overtly moralizing positions failed to acknowledge certain realities of sexuality—its messiness, diversity, and permeation by power, fear, and desire not easily averted. It does not seem very controversial to say that pleasure should not be realized at the expense of others' physical or emotional well-being, but the sticky business of sex makes the causal connections of harm and intention particularly difficult to trace. Social, sexual beings hurt and nurture each other through sex, in simple and complicated ways. What counts as harm is relative, and harm might not be sufficient to justify curtailing sexual knowledge, expression, or liberty. In the end, moralizing feminists refused to explore the resistant potential in the contradictory pleasures of female sexual exploration, and the fact that even pain can be part of the joy of sex.

The feud-like impasse that characterized feminist thinking about sex and ethics in the eighties and nineties was fueled by the fact that those who prioritized pleasure did not see the judgements inherent in their own positions, and those who were dedicated to the conscious elimination of oppression were not interested in the unconscious layers of sexual being, and the fact that sexuality can be a valuable source of embodied joy. Drives, desires, and embodied affairs cannot always be fully accommodated by talk of choice and agency. Yet their most subtle dimensions create the texture and motivation of ethical life.

The heat that characterized feminist conflicts over sexuality has subsided, and it appears that the fierce debates and assertions created interesting feminist political and cultural movements regarding the ethics of sexuality. The dwindling of the "sex wars" coincided with the demise of many nonacademic feminist intellectual spaces (feminist publications, publishing houses, and bookstores), particular demographic, geographic, and economic shifts, and mainstreaming of lesbian chic in the gay 1990s.

The sex wars were liveliest at the same time that the work of women of color and challenges to white feminists were also at the center of feminist intellectual and cultural life. Perhaps the lesson that gender and sexuality are always complicated by race and class helped undermine moralizing, and made it more difficult to think of sexuality as either simply empowering or oppressive. Feminist theorists began dealing with aging and AIDS, queer sex-positive culture exploded on the scene, and we faced increased political threats from the radical right. Perhaps other agendas became more important, or more appealing.

Poles of disagreement have shifted or dissolved, and it seems a loose consensus regarding the power and importance of sexual pleasure and exploration is present in feminism. The sex radicals of the eighties helped bring sex out of the American cultural closet and even made lesbian sex fashionable. Perhaps we've all just been brainwashed by capitalism. Perhaps we've become a bit more sexy and free. I like to think our attention to ethics and politics, and to justice and joy, has loosened the need to see moral life as a matter of conscious control. I believe we know the need for the fire that feeds ethical being. Like all other bodily ways, sexuality is part of the texture of moral life.

My feminist politics have always been interwoven with sexual choices, reflections, desires and identities. My own migration (I once was straight, now I'm not) has been shaped by a desire to enact feminist values—to "give free rein" to desires previously repressed and to "choose ways of being" that are not oppressive. Feminist ethical desires found sexual expression—how can ideas not engage the body? And my bodily experiences and responses have informed my beliefs. I do regard desire as a sometimes-conscious critical endeavor. Yet I know my sexuality is replete with complicating contradictions, sometimes energizing, sometimes baffling. My moral life is similar, but more so. I disappoint myself continually, and at times I seem entirely beyond my own control. I try to stay focused on the rewards of loving connection.

The intensity of joy and other rich affective experiences, including painful, confusing, and difficult feelings, create our ethical commitments to ourselves and others. They also save us from lives that would otherwise be empty, dull and uninspired. Knowing this makes me far less judgmental about my own and others' choices and desires, though I still find the uncritical conflations of eroticism and violence disturbing. I remain very interested in seeing what feminism has to offer those of us who are deeply attached to the importance of freedom and safety, justice and joy. Regarding ethics and politics, I have moved from a concern with working to eliminate oppression and harm to a more constructive interest in creating and uncovering ways to "forget" oppression, resist its force and trajectory, and diminish its seemingly thorough reach. I think of this as a shift toward an ethic of flourishing. As far as sexuality goes, and where doesn't it go, really, I believe this ethic includes a moral commitment to joy, including deeply physical joy.

Clearly, unless one is a hedonist, pleasure, physical thrill, or ecstasy cannot serve as ethical barometers, indicating the good or right. But they do have the potential to awaken and motivate love and commitments to flourishing, which inform our sense of ethics. We should therefore pay careful attention to them. Pleasure is not trivial, and is not a neutral response, an instance of which can be evaluated as simply consistent or inconsistent with values. Rather, feelings of pleasure are part of the complicated weave of ethical agency and selfhood. In fact, I would not be surprised if physical joy is crucial for the creative embodiment of the ethical. Even if it is only crucial for some of us, feminists should take to heart the ethical significance of joy and other ways of loving life.

Feminist Philosophy

If we are moved in ways that are not completely conscious, then taking embodiment to heart requires attention to the unconscious layers of ethical life. Interrogations of the deep sources and sites of ethical life need not lead us to reject ethical theorizing. Rather, ethical projects should be tempered by explicit, realistic, and tentative theories of embodied "psychological" being. Unfortunately, in feminist philosophy engagements with the psyche and analyses of ethics typically remain rather separate and compartmentalized. Although the questions and issues feminist thinkers ponder span the widest philosophical range, philosophers inherit boundaries and designations, such as the divide between "continental" and "analytic" philosophy, that are products of outdated masculinist traditions. Those boundaries discourage work that takes seriously both the importance of ethical theorizing and the significance of unconscious aspects of moral life. Continental thinkers are far more focused on the Hegelian branch of the history of philosophy, including poststructuralism and psychoanalytic thought, and analytic philosophers tend to identify with Kant, and to read in British and American traditions.

The field of feminist ethics is historically identified with analytic philosophy, although questions about ethics are often central to continental feminism as well. Feminist philosophers share questions regarding the character of moral agency, the relationships between norms and contexts, and transgressive political possibilities. Given those common questions, it is disappointing to see how little attention is paid across that analytic/continental divide. Insightful works such as Tina Chanter's *Ethics and Eros: Irigaray Rewrites the Philosophers* and Cynthia Willett's *Maternal Ethics and Other Slave Moralities* suffer from the authors' decisions not to engage relevant feminist work in ethical theory, including work on the nature of ethics, and limits of mothering as a moral model. In turn, continental feminists complain that analytic approaches are not sufficiently historical or psychoanalytic.

Traditionalist conceptions of Philosophy and its sacred texts, or reactionary conceptions of *real* philosophy prevent us from joining forces, and ultimately the loss is ours. Most feminist theorists read across a broad range, within and beyond our spheres of expertise, but this wider familiarity and interest is not often expressed in published work, and cultures of separate conferencing don't encourage much dialogue. But disparate schools of philosophical thought differ less than most disciplines do from each other, and in recent years many of us have become masters of interdisciplinarity—it is time for more border jumping within feminist philosophy.

Of course, there are deep and nontrivial philosophical differences embedded in different approaches, and these differences are rarely politically benign. Variations among approaches to ethics can correspond to very different beliefs about what knowledge, being, and meaning are, and about the very relevance of ethics. But for scholars who share political and practical agendas (which are also ethical agendas), differences can spark terrifically creative projects. The minimal normative edge of feminism is a good foundation for productive intellectual and political work across difference. When we look at lived feminist politics we see how important and dynamic, and how manageable some disagreements can be, especially over the long haul, and especially in such a patriarchal world.

A project that points in some promising directions is the book *Feminist Contentions: A Philosophical Exchange*, in which four brilliant feminist philosophers (Seyla Benhabib, Judith Butler, Drucilla Cornell, and Nancy Fraser) dialogue on feminism, philosophy, and postmodernism. A cluster of their contentions concerns normativity, and the ethical goals promoted or assumed by feminism. In the book's eight essays and counter-essays a central struggle develops between Drucilla Cornell's conception of an anti-normative "ethical feminism" and the more explicitly invested and theoretically weighty ethical norms endorsed by Fraser and Benhabib.

In "What Is Ethical Feminism?" Cornell argues for a feminism grounded in an attitude that she calls "the ethical," defined as "the aspiration to a nonviolent relationship to the Other and to otherness in the widest possible sense." Although she sees this aspiration as entailing attention to "what kind of person we become," she distinguishes it from *morality*, which she takes to be a system "that absolutely governs the 'right way to behave'" (78). Cornell's stated rejection of ethical norms and theories is thorough, so her position provides a helpful reference point for considering the logic and limits of anti-normative feminist positions. Additionally, her psychoanalytic approach takes seriously the often unconscious and inarticulable power of desire, drives, and emotions in shaping us as sexual and ethical beings. She identifies ethics not with a system of rules, but with an orientation that emerges through the distinction between self and other. Her view (echoing a range of positions, from Levinas to Gilligan) is that:

> the ethical is not a system of behavioral rules, nor a system of positive standards by which to justify disapproval of others. It is, rather, an attitude towards what is other to oneself (78).

Cornell's critique of ethical theory is threefold. She claims that ethical theory tends to be intolerant and moralizing, that nothing about ethics should be taken as absolute, and that normative and universal ethical theory cannot address what it means to take responsibility for what is unconscious. While she admits that all feminists make judgements, she believes we should be suspicious of any attempt to present judgements as integrated in a moral system. She asserts that the systematization of ethics excludes the crucial feminist task of continually re-imagining our own standards of right and wrong.

Although Cornell derides any determinable, theoretical reflections on morality, she also states that it is ultimately *for ethical reasons* that we should not construct ethical theories, because such attempts are likely to become moralistic and intolerant of difference. These worries about intolerance and moralizing echo libertarian feminists' claims that any judgements regarding sexuality are repressive, damaging, and a waste of feminist attentions. Putting aside for a moment the question of whether such an anti-normative normativity is even coherent, what should we make of this distaste for moralizing? Again, feminist rejection of moralizing makes sense, because questioning norms and rules expresses a resistant impulse that is central to feminism. Normativity is a universal tool of human modification, development, and repression, and it is often the first wave of fire in the journey to being a woman. Obvious and unspoken rules and moralities threaten us, mold us, and make us unfree. Even when it has good intentions, moralizing rests on the assumption that there is one correct way of thinking, acting, responding, or being, and that to depart from perfection is to undermine one's own humanity. Cornell takes legal theorist Catherine MacKinnon to represent "feminist moralizing," and feminist ethics, and therefore categorically rejects all ethical theorizing,

It is unfortunate that Cornell focuses on MacKinnon instead of engaging feminist philosophy and ethical theory that is critical of liberal conceptions of moral agency and that reject ethics of purity (such as the incredibly nuanced and influential work of María Lugones). While any values and evaluations put forth by feminists are normative and not merely descriptive, norms need not be absolute, universal, unified, or exclusive. Within philosophy, the field of feminist ethics has razed moral and theoretical edifices that take ethical agents to be rational robots, and that take ethics to be about rule-following. Work in feminist ethics is typified by theories that are sensitive to context, difference, particularity, and connection.

There is nothing defensible about ethical theory that presents norms as absolute and beyond debate. But presenting a system of apparently consistent and justifiable ethics need not imply that values, judgements, or principles are final or unrevisable. In fact, feminist ethics often achieves systematization through contingencies—articulating values that are contextual, socially situated, interested, and partial. The ethical imagination is expressed in art and poetry as well as argumentative prose. Does that not imply the potential benefits of the widest range of wisdom available concerning ethics? Theorizing searches for patterns of consistency and coherence in feminist ethical imaginings and beings about who we are, what we care about, and what we might become.

It is easy to forget that resistance to rules implies normative evaluations. Cornell eschews specific theoretical explorations of how we ought to be, and how we ought to be together, but even her critique of ethical theorizing rests on norms For example, she claims that intolerance is unethical, and that evil-mitigating gestures are crucial for feminist practice. She also believes that her version of the ethical demands that "we deconstruct the claim that we share an identity as women and that the differences between us are secondary" (85). I do not see sufficient foundation for these claims in her minimalist conception of the ethical, though I agree with her judgements. Difference is a starting point for feminism because of commitments to represent women, race, sexuality, and gender as accurately as possible, and to avoid silencing or otherwise harming women who are likely to disappear under the mirage of shared identity. These commitments are epistemic, political, and moral. As long as feminism includes the view that some actions, attitudes, and social systems are better than others, it is inconsistent with a rejection of norms. Instead, feminism requires normative ethical theory that is situated, psychologically sophisticated, and open to revision.

The Unconscious

Can theory or politics integrate essential feminist resistance to normativity with the necessity of feminist norms? It becomes possible to sit within that paradox when we appreciate the dynamic nature of feminism, and when we take seriously the unconscious layers of ethical life. I've used her as an negative example thus far, but Drucilla Cornell asks the million-dollar question about ethics and gendered/sexual agency: "How can we take responsibility for what is unconscious? (84)" (How are ethical relations informed by fantasies of Woman that are social, power-laden, and imparted through the development of identity? Is it possible to make unconscious patterns conscious, or to know when we are right about them? How does the position and experience of otherness call us to moral responsibility?)

To investigate these crucial questions, feminist philosophy can benefit from critical engagements with feminist scientific inquiries concerning the development of identity and moral agency, including the interwoven, relative formations of gender, race, class, and sexuality. The work of feminist psychoanalytic thinkers also helps prompt ethical explorations that plumb the depth of moral being. The more we know about the unconscious, the better we can theorize our moral possibilities and re-imagine our forms of life. Still, pondering the workings of the unconscious does not amount to resistance, or to justice. As

Benhabib and Fraser argue in *Feminist Contentions*, feminist struggles are not reducible to struggles to make unconscious patterns conscious, and struggles to change conscious and unconscious patterns are not reducible to a search for an accurate account of the unconscious.

While much of ethical life is beyond conscious control, our attempts to achieve transformation, and to reconfigure cultural understandings of Woman, are consciously strategized, discussed, and pursued. Political theorists need not become so preoccupied with judgement, with theorizing the psyche, or with working out the details of ethical life that we forget to inspire and notice change. Just as sexual ethics illuminate a crystalline tension between justice and joy, sexual politics produce bodies of knowledge that demand attention to life's choices.

If we take various bodies seriously, we see that feminist ethics are ethics of both justice and joy. If we give up the belief that ethics is an entirely conscious matter, and the belief that any formulation of norms or judgements is a threat, we can forge ethical possibilities that are both resistant and creative, and we can nurture joy alongside righteousness. The most compelling project of feminist ethics is the matter of building new cultures—not dreamy feminist utopias where consensus and uniformity rule, but varied spaces, practices, identities, and communities where resistant rhythms continue to develop. Heading there is simply a matter of slipping into the canyon.

Sisterwomanchainsaw

We (you and I) are walking in the woods. The air is cold and damp, but our pace and protective layers of wool and Goretex prevent us from feeling the chill. When it begins to snow we feel lucky to be outside, on this trail in Kentucky, in the first snow of fall. The leaves are gold, red, brown, and still green too, and the damp has soaked the tree bark black. The white snow against these colors is perfect—I want to savour the view like a painting. Clean white against crisp color. A rare combination.

We're hiking up the hill, boots gripping and sliding in damp chocolatey earth. Leaves are decomposing like muddy lace beneath our feet. Your nose is red, ice against my cheek, your breath a contrast of steam and sweetness. The air is still, and because the season has driven the critters out of sight in search of warmth, it almost seems that we are alone on this hillside, where life has slowed in anticipation of winter.

Then, as unexpected as thunder on a sunny day—gunshots—too close—and my heart drops like lead, into a pit of terror.

A wave of knowledge comes in an instant. It's Hunting Season.

We stop. We confer with glances, And in less than a minute we begin walking, now as fast as we can, back to the trailhead. The colors blur and earth becomes hard as we fill the air with chatter about wolves and other predators. To soften the intensity of my urgent need to put distance between myself and the guns, I tell you about the time I learned to shoot a forty-five. I also tell you about the guy in Wisconsin who shot his brother, who was sitting in a tree, because he mistook him for a deer. We recall movie images of black men being chased by the Klan through dense, humid forests. And when we're near the end of the trail we remember the chainsaw in the back of the truck.

We (you and I) want to scare the deer. We want to sabotage the hunt.

The pull-cord is tight, but after about twenty tries the damn chainsaw finally starts. Its loud metal whine cuts into the cold stillness, harsher and more sustained than any gunshot. I think: run away. I think: this is a warning. I think: I could take this chainsaw and rip right through their truck as though it were a cartoon image. My face is burning and zinc-colored smoke is engulfing us, but the urgent vibration of the resonant machine swells my pounding heart. I'm afraid the hunters will come and get us, and I fear their guns, but we let the chainsaw roar for as long as we can stand it. We want to scare the animals. To interrupt the predator's strategic silence. We want the deer to run to safety.

No one emerges angrily, or frightened, from the woods. You kill the engine, and the silence rings across our small universe. On the way home you seem to savour the lack of noise, but I am preoccupied. I cannot find words to describe my sense of failure. Of embarrassment and jubilation. Then we (you, then I) begin to talk. About how I am always convincing you to do silly things. About how when deer flee in fright, they are more vulnerable to hunters. About how the flesh of one deer can feed a family for weeks. About what it means when a violent practice turns into a sport. About women hunters and national forests.

We don't know if there was anything sensible we could have done to make good on our compassion for the deer who live in those Kentucky woods. Yet we don't want to let go of our sense that we did something to disrupt an institution that we disdain. That in telling the story, we might figure out how to better enact compassion and rage. That in my sense of myself, and in our sense of us, it matters that we are not content to let it be.

Codeword: Diversity

I have always been cynical about talk of "diversity" on campuses and in institutional settings. Programs that promote diversity trumpet inclusion as a panacea, but inclusion is measured superficially, usually through institutional or wide-lens statistics. Inclusion alone does not address real differences of power and the deep effects of history. After all, looking with a wide lens, plantations were diverse. The racial politics of a place cannot be measured in statistics, or aesthetics.

Yet there is an understanding of diversity, and a way of approaching it, that can be quite helpful. Talk of diversity can be an institutional ploy for avoiding deeper change, but inside and outside institutions diversity can also function as an *ethical* goal. "Diversity" is often used as code for pluralism, especially (but not only) racial or ethnic pluralism. *To value diversity in an ethical sense is to believe that relevant and unfairly excluded others ought to be included.* Valuing diversity is a way of encouraging groups and gatherings that are representative, "multicultural," and in other ways preferable to uniform groups. Those who value diversity in this sense may pay attention to demographics, assessing the politics of a gathering (and therefore their own comfort levels) by noting the appearance of the people who are part of it. The politics of a place cannot really be measured by appearances, of course, but those who value diversity believe something about appearances is politically relevant.

Diversity is valued because it is a visual mark of certain political commitments (against prejudice, and for inclusivity). It is also valued because of what it can bring to a social space, such as more democratic participation, better representation, and useful input from a variety of perspectives. Those who value diversity believe diversity in the realm of appearances can be an important step toward better institutions and better cultures.

> *On our way out of the meeting Julissa turns to me and asks "What did you think?" I tell her that I thought the panel went really well, that I was glad to see such a big turnout on a rainy night. "Not very diverse, though," she says, and I agree. We head for the cafe to meet up with the rest of the gang, to strategize and develop a better outreach plan.*
>
> *The committee that runs this group is fairly diverse, but the larger membership is composed mostly of white progressives. Outreach has been a real challenge—when we have a Latina speaker, the Latinos show up, and our audiences are more black when we meet uptown, but it is difficult to generate interest across predictable groupings. Maybe our agenda is perceived as a white thing, even though it's poor people and people of color who are most directly affected by the policies we're working to change. Some of us decide to create a task force to focus on diversity. Others plan a media event on immigrants' rights. A few people think all this worrying about diversity is a waste of time—what matters is whether we are working on the right issues, and toward positive change.*

Noticing a lack of diversity is a good way to name the fact that a group is too uniform. That very assessment, "too uniform," indicates that institutions and gatherings should include a certain amount of difference, or certain forms of difference. The "should" may be a matter of law, or a claim that certain differences are valuable in their own right. Segregationist and sexist histories make certain uniformities (all white folks, all men) inherently suspect. Uniformity might indicate exclusionary practices or attitudes, or the fact that the group is not interested in changing. The rhetoric of diversity can refer to a range of qualities (race, gender, physical ability, and sometimes sexuality), but talk of diversity is most commonly used to highlight racial and ethnic diversity. In historically white contexts, racial diversity, when it is present in most levels of the hierarchy, is taken to indicate that physical and cultural differences are tolerated, and that a place is not particularly unwelcoming to people of color. The American military is an example of the kind of institution considered appropriately diverse in that sense.

Diversity need not be racial, or even visible. Nearly any uniform group includes a diversity of perspectives and cultures, and widely different values and histories. And any collectivity, as meaningful as it might be, is a product of social norms that can shift and change. Institutional goals of diversity focus on visible or obvious differences— differences that have been recognized as significant by law or by culture. But focusing on visible differences maintains the myth that the most important forms of difference are visible. That view gives the impression that members of groups have more in common than they really do, and obfuscates the differences within the collective.

Diversity names a fairly superficial state of affairs. As an institutional goal, diversity is meant to address the effects of explicit and implicit rules of exclusion: white-only or white supremacist policies, sexism, laws against gender nonconformity, inaccessibility of space to disabled people, prohibitions on displays of lesbian and gay love. The differences marked by diversity are deeply social (their meanings and significance are social, not biological truths) but they are also material and bodily, and therefore visible. When institutions promote diversity, their success is measured in statistics.

Beyond statistical assessments of diversity, talk of diversity is used as code to indicate that people of color are present and welcome. Although it still relies on fairly superficial demographic assessments, as an ethical goal diversity indicates valuing social spaces that are pluralist, representative, and fair. Diversity names a social good, but unlike justice, it does not assume that what we have in common is always more significant than what makes us different and distinct. Diversity is not as fundamental as justice—it is valuable because (or when) it is just. But diversity can also be valuable because of what it brings in its own right.

Diversity in Institutions

Diversity is encouraged by the law insofar as it serves as an indicator of fair institutional practices regarding protected groups. Corporations, government agencies, and universities use the language of diversity to promote tolerance and respect, and to protect themselves from legal challenges.

Diversity in institutions can be a sham. Programs that promote diversity can give the impression that members of formerly excluded groups are valued, even when there are no efforts made to meet their specific needs, or to integrate them into leadership positions where their presence and input might have the greatest effect. Diversity is rhetorically promoted in contexts where there is no real desire to encourage the fruitful change and growth that can emerge from pluralism. The ethics of diversity are therefore not allowed to deeply shape the system, or alter the way it functions in the world. It is easy to be cynical about institutional calls for diversity.

Take for example fictional City U. A state-funded university, it is run by a conservative mostly-white administration and a conservative mostly-white board of trustees. It has a faculty that is mostly white, and a mixed student body. That is, most students are white, but about 20 percent are African American, and although there are very few Native Americans or Latinos, there are a fair number of Asian American and international students on campus. The administrative staff is mixed, and most service and custodial workers are black. Through its website and promotional materials, the institution represents itself as a welcoming place for nonwhite students. Diversity is promoted through cultural and multicultural events and celebrations, and the language of diversity is omnipresent in common spaces and administrative rhetoric.

Top-ranking administrators at City U include one or two African Americans, and there are a few black and Asian student leaders as well.

African American Studies is a strong academic department, and some of its members are internationally renowned. But there are many academic departments that remain completely white, and overall, black undergraduates tend to gravitate toward "practical" majors, rather than majors that lead to graduate studies. Student social life is intensely segregated. If you look at classrooms, programmatic alliances, and paychecks, you'll see that what might look like a healthy blend separates along predictable lines.

Is this place diverse? There is no denying that when one walks around campus, things feel diverse. Compared to most private liberal arts colleges, for example, this campus has a visible and thriving black culture. But the institution's affirmative action policies are directed at the macro and not the micro level, and many members of the university community voice frustration with the conservativism and the racial politics of the place. Talk of diversity is used to promote appearances, but appearances are a matter of shallow aesthetics and statistics. To really value diversity at the deepest levels of an institution is to welcome the possibility of change and transformation, because diversity represents some significant and positive difference from the uniform status quo. Most institutions are interested in being fair, or in following the law, but not many institutions seek and welcome unpredictable change. We should not be surprised when challenging demands are channeled into diversity programs that leave fundamental disparities unchanged.

Yet statistical diversity (the fact that there are a fair number of black students on campus, for example) can provide the conditions for enacting more effective politics of difference, and those who value diversity as an ethical goal can take advantage of statistical diversity. At City U, a committed administrator in the College of Practical Technology could create a program to recruit black students from local high schools, brokering support by using the institution's pro-diversity rhetoric. The program could successfully shift the demographics within that area of study, significantly increasing the number of African Americans in the field. Graduates of that program might become leaders in the broader community as well.

Perhaps integrating more black students into majors that bring them fully into the middle class (a kind of economic affirmative action) is not revolutionary change. Certainly achieving diversity is not all that is needed to confront racism and its astounding legacies. But I agree with Cornel West that "Affirmative action is not the most important issue for black progress in America, but it is part of a redistributive chain that must be strengthened if we are to confront and eliminate black poverty" (96). Universities and other institutions that distribute economic privilege are key links in that chain, and the function and effects of diversity in those contexts are complex matters.

Calls for diversity that come down from above in the form of buzzwords and poster initiatives may be nothing but attempts to make it look like an institution is doing the right thing. But whether or not an institution is doing the right thing, the people within it can work strategically to make the most of the diversity that lurks beneath categorical divisions (such as divisions between faculty, students, and pink- and blue-collar workers). If there is something valuable about racial and cultural diversity, the diversity that exists in any setting can be a starting place for a more democratic and inclusive community. As long as internal policies are fair, with careful strategizing even superficial diversity can be mobilized to impact deeper levels of the system.

Diversity in Life

Along with our lives in institutions, we create the social world by gathering with others. We gather for political meetings, for fun and to be entertained. We gather for spiritual community, for learning, and for creative projects. These gatherings are not necessary in the ways work and school are necessary, yet we seek them out and dedicate ourselves to them. Voluntary and intentional (even when they occur in institutions), social gatherings are often our most treasured forms of association. When diversity is promoted there, it is more often an expression of ethics, and not a strategy for avoiding lawsuits.

As an ethical term, diversity conveys a statement of values and an aesthetic diagnosis. Still, what looks diverse to me might look too uniform to you. Diversity is nearly always a subjective and context-specific designation.

A group of people who live in a racially and culturally diverse city convene to form a political organization in response to a local and national crisis. Most have experience working in political groups of some sort—they are professionals and activists. The group is mostly white, but it includes people of color, lesbians and gay men, older folks, and disabled people, and the leadership of the group is mixed. Although the explicit political agenda of the group is not a "racial" issue (perhaps they are working on abortion rights, or environmental issues), the group decides that their agenda should include working to make their own group more diverse. They plan to make alliances with groups and community leaders who represent people of color. A commitment to diversity is included in their mission statement.

An illustrator's work characteristically features cartoon-like drawings of people and animals. He believes it is always important to represent diversity, so he creates images that include characters with various skin tones, body shapes, and hairstyles. He knows there is something a bit false and contrived in the representation, but for him that is part of the project, and part of the pleasure. He enjoys drawing the kind of world he thinks he'd like to see. His work attracts a diverse array of clients, and he is especially pleased when people who are not white are drawn to his work, because he believes that indicates that he is doing something right.

A black woman and a white woman who have been friends for years occasionally throw parties together. They both prefer hanging out in racially mixed groups, and over the years they have collected a lengthy list of people (black, white, and beyond) to invite to their gatherings. Their parties feature black music, dancing, and lots of food. They consider their parties successful when a "healthy mix" of guests shows up. When mostly white people show up, the two women usually feel the party is a little boring.

In evaluating a scene (What did you think of the meeting? What did you think of the party?) someone who values diversity may be guilty of promoting and seeking out a fairly aesthetic and superficial goal. Yet deep values that inform how one wants the world to look, the kind of society one seeks out.

My dictionary defines diversity as the "quality, state, fact, or instance of being diverse; difference," and "variety." Clearly difference alone cannot be morally valuable, because it just means something is unlike something else. Valuing diversity implies valuing certain differences and particularities—what is relevant will depend on the context and the project at hand. Behind diversity as an ethical value can be the belief that certain forms of variety (such as an ethnic pluralism that reflects the local population) are necessary for a good political process, or for the kinds of results the group is seeking. Ethics of diversity do at least minimally rely on identity politics, because they ask if the "right" people are present, though they require openness to the process that unfolds out of pluralism and democratic engagement. Commitments to diversity therefore have an aesthetic component. How can they not, if they are partially about how one believes the world should "look"? But as with diversity in institutions, the matter of the mix is only the beginning.

Difficulties of Diversity

Even for those who value diversity, the challenges presented by difference can cause conflict. Differences in culture and values, and even physical differences, can be profoundly threatening because they can disrupt beliefs that seem foundational. Many psychoanalytic and psychological traditions identify the challenge of difference as the most basic and formative of human traumas, because it originates in the recognition of the self, and enculturation through language. Audre Lorde believed acknowledging deep fears of difference was key to political and emotional progress for everyone. She wrote, "I urge each one of us here to reach down into that deep place of knowledge inside herself and touch that terror and loathing of any difference that lives there. See whose face it wears" (113). Interactions across difference resonate deeply in the body and the psyche. That is why they can be so attractive, and so despised.

We have all inherited horrible legacies of hatred. Even outside institutions, it can be difficult to trust calls for diversity that come from the mouths of people with privilege. For those with abstract commitments to diversity, it can be difficult to know what forms of diversity are best in a particular situation, and when difference becomes deeply challenging, it can be difficult to follow through on abstract commitments. Sometimes people think they want diversity, but they are not really prepared to deal with difference. Tokens are welcome because they make the place look more diverse and spice things up a bit. But their input cannot go anywhere when there are no strategies for or commitments to encouraging pluralism, and allowing the change that inevitably results from diversity. Even in the company of the best intentions, when those who usually run things or those with privilege have not done their homework, their attempts to promote diversity can feel like tokenism. Diversity will nearly always bring challenges that cannot be anticipated in advance, so an ethical commitment to diversity is a real moral commitment to pluralism, and to fair processes. If the tokens are committed to the project at hand, and to diversity, they can sometimes find ways to take advantage of their position to educate others, and to create bridges and policies that will ultimately move local politics of difference beyond tokenism.

Diversity does not require just any pluralism. It demands the inclusion of relevant and unfairly excluded others, and a community in which difference is a site of exchange, not repulsion. Exactly who the relevant others are will vary from context to context. An unfortunate use of diversity discourses uses "diversity" as an excuse for laissez faire politics, as though if we value diversity, we must respect any opinion or perspective as valid, or equal to all other ideas. But simplistic relativism is not unique to diversity as an ethical value—justice, rights-talk, and even compassion are used as excuses for a nonjudgemental stance that is incapable of criticizing harmful views. It is not difficult to show that simplistic relativism holds no water as a moral view, but it can be incredibly difficult to argue with people who are convinced that any judgement is tyranny.

When you look at your group and think "we need more diversity," it's not a sign of failure, but it is a sign that you have probably already created something that is likely to attract a limited group of people. In that case, if you want diversity, something fundamental in your approach must change. Contexts can be perceived as exclusive, unwelcoming, or uninteresting to "others" because of who is already present or involved, the location, what it costs to attend (in monetary or symbolic terms), or because of the traditions the gathering references. Sometimes just changing locations or advertising strategies can draw a more diverse community. If you want more black people to attend your pow-wow, for example, you may need to do special outreach, or to invite a prominent African Americans to participate as leaders and special guests.

Diversity is no panacea, as a state of affairs, an ethical value, or a democratic strategy. At most it is good starting point for fruitful and engaged pluralism. Diversity simply *is*—relevant others are always "present"—so we can benefit from the political and aesthetic favors it offers. In America (and nearly everywhere else) the idea of a monoculture is a media-driven fantasy. Even the American family is commonly a mishmash of cultural influences. Given the diversity in our realities, there is no reason to apologize for preferring a diverse world. Diversity is a form of human beauty. Valuing diversity includes recognizing that "us" and "we" are inherently diverse concepts, and appreciating the multiplicity that exists within any collectivity. Mindfulness concerning the depth of difference and particularity in the midst of connection and similarity can move us beyond divisive distinctions.

It does not take a rocket scientist to figure out that most social exclusions are unjust, or deeply linked to injustice. As a codeword for openness, diversity can provides a banner under which we can form coalition, create resistance, and transform dominating cultures and institutions. When we work together across difference, as partners in close proximity, we cannot help but effect change. Justice requires thoughtful and compassionate openness to such change.

The King of Whiteness

This a story about a girl who chooses whiteness over knowledge. That white woman is me. When I say that I'm white, I supposedly mean there are no folks of color in my family or my family's history, as far as I know, or as far as it matters. In the naming of my own racial identity, I apply a detestable principle, the one drop rule, to tell you that I am pure—with no colored blood. But where does a family history begin?

Is my application of the one drop rule so seamless? What if, contrary to fact, I had a great aunt Ella, married into the family, who was Chinese, who taught me her language, and who loved me like a grandmother?

More likely, my dark immigrant family arrived in New York uncertain of their social status, yet certain that their skin was the color of olives, not eggplants (as they came to describe the skin of this country's former slaves). How many generations, how many miles from the center of the city does it take to whitewash ethnicity? I claim the generations before me as "white" as though that's the way those peasants from Sicily and Czechoslovakia saw themselves. As though whiteness were timeless.

Stories of how the Irish became white aside, it's clear that Europe matters. No matter that the successes and superiorities associated with Europe resulted from nearly accidental combinations of technology, luck, and evil. European powers set out to rule the world, and made the pale face a sign of power, money, and knowledge. This despite other associations of that face with stupidity, aesthetic inferiority, and moral decrepitude.

What is this identity "white" that marks my body, that I (here, now) cannot help but take as a name? I am white, yet I believe that in some other universe of meaning and power, things could be otherwise. In my own life, I don't really know how to make sense of this belief.

Since I've come to understand whiteness not as an attribute or quality, but as a category that maintains its own power, I've longed for an alternative. Just as I moved myself (or so it seemed) from straight girl to lesbian so many years ago, I wish I could abandon whiteness—this form of personhood that signifies oppression—and forge an identity that marks, with the simplicity of a name or a haircut, just how fucked up I think racism is. There are moments when I agree with those who say that the elimination of racism requires a flight from whiteness. But to where? When I consider what it would mean to not be white, my political conscience becomes uneasy (wannabe!), and my imagination fails me.

I think: I can only hope for a miracle. I wonder: what do I stand to lose?

Yes, this is all about me. That's a white-people habit, a middle-class habit—to think and talk as though we deserve being the center of attention. It's downright American. But what does it really matter what my identity suggests to the world, as long as the lives of people who aren't white, rich, or normal are harmed by the norms of race, class, and gender?

I hate when men say they are not really men. What a lie, I think. If you're not really a man, why can't I see your inability to reside in privilege? Shouldn't the whole world be able to see your discomfort in conforming to the rules of manhood? Let's see your privilege crack you in two! Let's see you give it up, brother! Until I know you're for real, don't tell me you're not really a man. You have no idea.

My friend Suzanne was born a man. Before she became Suzanne, the guy she was participated fully in manhood. He was married, had children, and was a member of the U.S. Air Force (she tells me that many trans women are former military men). Suzanne became a woman in ways that are visible because she felt like a woman inside—in ways that only she knew. *I hate when men say they're not really men.* When Suzanne says she didn't feel like a man before, I don't mind. Something has convinced me that before she became a woman, Suzanne could not abide the norms of manhood. As a man, they were destroying her.

Whiteness is not destroying me. I can't say that I always felt white, because I just always felt normal. As soon as I knew that not everyone was white, I knew that I was at the top of the heap. I knew that I had been born lucky. There were other ways that I felt like a freak, different from the people around me. I would rather read than play kickball. I could communicate with animals. I thought prejudice was bad, and I protested and sometimes cried when my family told racist jokes. None of these qualities ever made me feel that I was not white. Lucky.

Whiteness, education, and money help get me just about everything I want in the world, including love and good health. Although I feel little kinship with most white people, whiteness is not a prison house for me. It is easy to be white. Do men feel this way about their privilege? Are you laughing at me?

I have very little knowledge about what it means to not be white, and whatever I might have to say about not being white could be said much better by someone who is not white. So what makes me think I have anything worthwhile, anything worth your time, to say about being white? About what I think about my own whiteness?

Wait: In order to say something about whiteness I begin thinking about not-white. Why is that so much easier than thinking about whiteness itself? Because white is nothing. White is everything, and there is absolutely nothing redeemable about whiteness. White is history, context, domination. And me. I'm white.

But I'm getting ahead of myself. This is a story about the standpoint of whiteness. I offer it to provide some fragments, to add these patterns and contradictions to the narratives we construct together regarding race, gender, and desire. Is it at all worth trying to understand something about race through the lens of gender? You be the judge:

A drag ball was being held as a fundraiser for AIDS organizations, and Kristin and I assumed there would be a handful of drag kings among the scores of queens. Kristin is big and beautiful. Her mother is Filipina, her father is from Puerto Rico (she says, I'm not sure if he's really Puerto Rican, I was always told he was Spanish). She arrived at my house in a tailored black suit. I wore my thrift store suit, cufflinks, white shirt buttoned to the neck. Kristin used mineral spirits to apply a mustache to her face. I could get away with just using mascara to highlight my own mustache and sideburns. She showed me a trick—darkening the eyebrows—and we both plastered our hair straight back with lots of goo.

Oh my god, I said.

We look like Chicano homeboys, she said.

Dark sunglasses on, and we hit the street. I felt like Danny DeVito next to Jimmy Smits.

This is who I've always wanted to be, she said.

Shit, I thought, I'm scared.

There is the danger of walking out of one's home dressed like a member of the wrong gender. There is the danger of looking like a hood in a neighborhood crawling with cops. There is the danger of looking Latino in a neighborhood where white yuppies, Appalachians, African Americans, and assorted queers coexist in an uneasy tension. What did I fear? Getting caught.

The car felt safe. It felt right to be cruising through the city, sitting on the passenger side as Kristin drove, windows open, my head bobbing to the beat as Celia Cruz led us into the night. When we reached the center of the city the first miracle occurred.

We slowed for a traffic light. Two black girls—teenagers—were walking along the sidewalk on my side of the street. By instinct, I smiled at them. I was completely unprepared for the miracle that met me on the face of the younger girl. The smile she gave me in response was completely open and inviting. It was the kind of smile I've only seen on the faces of women who are flirting with me and confident of their conquest. It is not a look that I have ever gotten from or given to a stranger.

She liked me.

I remembered how I looked. And realized: She thinks I'm a guy.

I thought, This is how straight people flirt with each other all of the time!

I thought, She did not think I was white, as we drove to the fancy banquet hall.

There is another version of this story—the version in which I make Kristin stop the car. We join those girls instead of going on to the draggy fags, and I spend the evening making that girl laugh. But I'm not telling that story right now. I'm telling the one that happened in time and space, not in the gossamer of imagination. I'm telling you the story in which the clueless drag king is offered redemption. And refuses.

Drag queens call themselves illusionists. Get close to one, and it's usually easy to see that she's really a guy. Though I create illusions of identity all of the time, I didn't think about the power of illusion until I accidentally became a brown man for an evening.

The second miracle involved the male gaze. Kristin and I were the only girls in boy drag at this Midwestern extravaganza. It seemed that hardly anyone was fixed on the action onstage as queers milled about the ballroom, costumed for pleasure. In the dark cabaret scene we still passed. We hung out in the back of the hall, arms crossed, occasionally relaxing the stance to smoke. We watched the parade of monstrous divas sashay to the stage, we shook our heads at the poorly executed lip synching, we took in the full glory of the long curvaceous legs on the fake ladies. By the time the awards ceremony started, we had found a groove. And who noticed us?

White boys in black leather.

The look was clear and direct. Sexual, fierce, but not threatening. I felt like a curious, inexperienced boy, peering into the edge of a culture that I longed to join. I felt like an adventurous seasoned fag sizing up the possibilities. I thought some white leather daddy could show this homeboy a very good time, if I were sufficiently willing. All alongside the exoticization and arrogance that likely lurked behind that wanting whiteboy gaze.

I thought, I am getting much more action as a Latino than I ever get as a white dyke.

I felt a surge of potential in one of those moments that is ubiquitous in queer experience, where gender seems to melt away and we all are just beings with a wide range of genitalia and facial hair and nose shapes and skin tones and the bodily truths are intoxicating. Squint and that guy walking toward you has a genderless face. Blink and that tall woman's dark skin is only the play of light on flesh. Close your eyes and there are no signifiers. Just scent and motion and an open range of connection, repulsion, and transformation.

The third miracle began with the phone ringing. We were in position near the back wall when a service phone near Kristin's head began to ring. Phone ringing? In the middle of a party? Is someone calling?

Kristin moved to pick up the phone. With a sudden perception that crackled I became aware of the uniformed staff patrolling the party. Were they protecting the queers, or monitoring us? As Kristin brought the phone to her ear they descended on her— white men in uniform ready to wrestle this troublemaker to the ground and prevent the inappropriate use of a service phone. They were *mad*. They were *serious*. And they assumed that the colored guy picking up the phone was up to no good.

It broke my heart, in that flash of a moment, to see Kristin's look melt from pure cool to startled nervousness. What, she said. What did I do wrong?

Later I thought that maybe it had been the Virgin Mary on the phone. See, stupid (she said), I'm giving your sorry ass, your lucky ass, three visions that you have the privilege and misfortune to ignore every damn day. She wanted to let me know I had one last chance. She provided the miracles, but I failed. I never got to hear her Semitic wisdom, and I blame the white men in uniform.

This is who I always wanted to be.

✳ ✳ ✳

The bartender notices me from the corner of his eye, and immediately makes clear his distaste, his suspicion. He thinks if he ignores me, maybe I'll go away. I think, he thinks I'm Latino. I think, he's being mean to me. I think something bad is going to happen.

I know that when I open my mouth I will commit myself to a gender. I realize that with a lilt and a smile I can escape back to whiteness and exit this moment of awkward fear. Or I can test out my boy voice and remain threatening to this poor racist bartender who's probably making only five bucks an hour.

I could also just avoid the whole dilemma by pulling out my money and pointing to a beer. But I don't.

I smile sweetly. I find my feminine register. I let him see my whiteness and my gender, let him see that I'm not scary. I order a whitegirl beer, and in gratitude and solidarity I leave a big tip.

I commit the original sin of whiteness. I let go the knowledge.

Getting Closer: On the Ethics of Knowledge Production

What do we need to know in order to move toward a better world? How can those of us who are paid to produce knowledge orient our work and direct the fruits of our labor according to our best values?

Along with dramatic strides toward global democracy, our historical era is marked by a mind-boggling amount of human suffering and destruction of the nonhuman world. Producers of knowledge ought to take this state of affairs to be a crisis that calls for focused attention and the development of useful tools. As our moral reach has grown wider and increasingly impersonal, theory has grown less useful, less interested in being useful to people who do not make their living reading and writing theory, less interested in being useful in our own lives outside the work of spinning theory. Concerning "ethical agency," the distances between theory and everyday life is too wide, and we ought to question our own comfort in that distance, especially our professional comfort in that distance.

Within a diverse community of knowledge producers, there is a wide range of desires concerning our work, knowledge, and the ethics that shape our lives. Yet in the midst of all of this difference, perhaps

Presented as the keynote address for the Michigan State University Philosophy Graduate Student Conference, October 2000.

there is a strand of resemblance from which we might wonder whether our work is sufficiently contributing to the world we want, and if it's not, whether there is anything we can do about it.

What should our work be, here and now, as producers of knowledge? Can academic conversations really help us figure out how to make a better world, how to be better people? Can ethics? Political theory? Can science? What does it mean, here and now, to engage in the activity of knowledge production with integrity? And can philosophy itself help us answer these questions?

I am aware that I ask about the ethics of knowledge production from the privileged position of a tenured academic, within an institutional economy that is increasingly profit-driven, in which the bulk of sustaining labor is done by underpaid service workers, by graduate student teachers, and by adjunct professors who lack job security and benefits, and who have little incentive or time to work on research projects of any sort. The systems of scarcity and exploitation that shape academic life and educational institutions in the United States are probably the first things we need to address when thinking about the ethics of knowledge production. If we have not already lost the battle, academic professionals need to get much more involved in local struggles against the corporate university if we hope to work with integrity, and within institutions that we do not despise.

But if I agitate against the exploitation of graduate students and adjunct professors, does that mean I have to give up my excellent job, with my comfortable teaching load, money for travel, and time off to do research and to write?

That unappealing question brings me back to the topic at hand: how to bridge what sometimes seems to be an incredibly distant relationship between ethics and action, between knowledge and life.

I want my knowledge-producing labor to be in the service of a better world, the good life for all, a smarter society, a healthier planet, a more sensual, arousing culture, a life-loving, peaceful, happy, clearheaded, okay world. Yet, I must admit that even as a professional ethicist, and as someone with an overdetermined tendency to want to do the right thing, it is often terribly difficult to follow my own best philosophical advice. This dramatic disconnect makes me wonder if my labor, especially my theory making labor, is severely misguided, if I'm asking the wrong questions, looking in the wrong places, speaking the wrong language, seeking out the wrong co-conspirators.

This problem is far too big to address here. But perhaps it would be helpful to focus on a particular aspect of my own moral failure: a form of moral distance. More and more, as members of global postindustrial economies, we are in close ethical proximity with people, communities, nonhuman species, and ecosystems that are very distant from us, geographically, affectively, and epistemically. Our current lives are so enmeshed with the lives of distant people, places, plants and animals, that it is ridiculous to even pretend that we have an emotional or epistemic connection with our moral worlds. We are members of economic and environmental communities too large, too diverse to even imagine.

What might it mean to promote the good of a community you cannot even hold in your imagination? Some of the most pressing, vexing ethical issues that face privileged folks right now are those in which, if we are to do the right thing, we must stretch across enormous epistemic chasms. If we take this distance seriously, we find several areas where traditional conceptions of ethical life fail us:

1) **Problems that result from developments in technology, population growth, and a world of pollution gone haywire, especially as these impact on the more than human world: the problems addressed by the discourse of environmental ethics.**

Because harms to nonhuman entities are often not analogous to typical human centered concerns, any claims of harm are subject to significant skepticism. It follows that facts about harm to nonhumans is not usually inherently persuasive as cause for moral concern. Although the fields of environmental ethics and the environmentalist sciences attempt to address these ontological and epistemic questions concerning how to "count" nonhuman interests, accompanying shifts in understandings of moral agency have not been fully explored.

Also, environmental ethics as it is currently conceived tells us quite a lot about how bad things are, but does very little to investigate the fact that changes in behavior require extraordinary amounts of motivation when a network of forces benefit from the maintenance of destructive practices and ignorance. To what does "environmental ethics" refer even when our ecological agency is less like a vector and more like smoke?

2) **Problems that result from histories of people exploiting other people in the name of nation, or in the name of men, or whatever institutions or networks of powerhouses have benefited and continue to benefit from the extraction of life, labor, and material goods from the darker, femmier, "dumber," less technologically advanced, poorer people. We might lump these together as the problems of "postcolonial ethics," or the politics of social embodiment—what might be optimistically considered the concerns of twenty-first century feminism.**

Concerning these problems, evidence that humans are harmed by seemingly democratic practices is subject to unique forms of skepticism, and can always be argued away by some other appeal to human rights or interests. For example, consider procapitalist arguments for exploitation in the interest of increasing "jobs," a move that seems to justify nearly any form of harm these days. Again, knowing the "facts" about harms is not enough.

In general (and I take feminist philosophy and critical race theory to be exceptions here), philosophy has not really taken seriously the question of how we can be responsible *to* histories that we are not responsible *for*, although this is one of the most important moral and political questions of our day. Philosophy also has not adequately acknowledged the fact that such questions are inevitably addressed from specific locations within massive, diverse, deeply segregated moral and political cultures.

3) **Problems that result from global capitalism.**

Contemporary moral agents are embedded in economic relationships with people we cannot even imagine. Our money and therefore our
desires and our work are mobilized in the service of the exploitation
of people all over the place, from midtown Manhattan to Malalaling.
The people who make our clothes and grow our food are so far away
from us, there is no way it can be meaningfully said that we "have a
relationship" with them, though we are related in complicated webs of
interdependence. Sartre's mid-twentieth-century problem of dirty
hands was nothing compared to this.

This problem is not just a result of physical distance. It might also
be argued that the people who do our dirty work right around the corner are even farther away than ever before. Think of how much you
know about who washes the toilets where you work. In the university
where I teach, the custodial staff works mostly at night, so professors
and daytime students only occasionally even see them in passing.

For all of these problems, it is not possible to clearly map causality,
so blame is not a useful way to motivate a sense of moral responsibility,
or alternative strategies. Even when we know whom to blame—whose
fault it is, or who is benefiting knowingly or unknowingly—there are
not obvious ways to turn knowledge into action. This is why we often
feel so impotent and ethically confused. Even when we want to do the
right thing, it seems as though the world is conspiring against us. More
profoundly, knowledge about facts—even facts about clear harms—is
not enough to motivate ethical responses.

You may *know,* because you are an unusually aware person, that it is
nearly impossible in the United States to buy food in a grocery store
without supporting multinational supercorporations. You may believe
corporations fix prices, exploit farmers and farm workers, and are currently fighting for the right to include genetically engineered products in
virtually everything you eat. Even if you know you are supporting a
harmful industry when you go grocery shopping, few people know

exactly where their food comes from, who grew it, and whether the workers were exposed to dangerous chemicals in the process. We do not know if the seeds from which it was grown were stolen and patented by some corporation, or any of the other socioeconomic and environmental details embedded in the production of what sustains us. But is it even enough to know where our food comes from, and what is in it?

Most traditional philosophical views assume the relationship between knowledge and responsibility to be straightforward. When we know of a clear causal connection between our choices and harm to others, there is a direct, self-evident duty to alleviate that harm (when such remedies are possible), and to refrain from causing further harm. Utilitarians, deontologists, and virtue theorists agree: rationality demands that, if we want to do the right thing, and there is not much of significance competing for our attention, the right action will be obvious and attractive. In the ideal case, when we want to do the right thing, facts alone provide moral motivation. When facts show that something we value is harmed, and that our actions are contributing to that harm, knowledge is supposedly sufficient to motivate us to act so as to stop causing harm, to do the right thing.

It is not surprising, then, that popular and academic environmentalist discourses assume a direct, reliable relationship between knowledge and morally motivated action. This is why statistics on global warming are presented as though the facts themselves imply direct responsibilities on the part of offending industries, societies whose economic prosperity depends on polluting forces, and consumers of fossil fuels. The assumption is that if we know the harm that fossil fuel consumption causes, and we want to promote a healthy environment, the course of action is obvious: we will reduce our consumption. When environmentalists (including environmentalist scientists) inform the public about the relationships between CO_2 emissions and climate change, they hope to ignite a sense of moral responsibility in consumers, industries, and governing bodies.

Why, then, do facts about global warming appear grossly inadequate to provide the moral motivation to significantly change consumer habits or demands, even among so-called committed environmentalists? When the harm in question is not direct harm to existing humans, but diffuse effects on nonhuman individuals, species and communities, or future generations of humans, or when it is impossible to map a clear causal relationship between actions and harms, even to humans, a direct relationship between knowledge (about harms) and action (to alleviate or refrain from causing further harms) simply does not emerge.

Traditional ethical theory, as well as most commonsense post-Enlightenment understandings of moral life, provide very little to help with these difficult dimensions of contemporary ethical life. I for one feel I know almost nothing about how to be a good postcolonial global citizen, how to be a person with integrity (and not an insanely obsessed crusader) in the face of these kinds of moral problems. Am I a complete failure as a human being, or is there some deep and problematic disconnect between theory and reality, between "ethics" and life?

The matters I address here challenge traditional understandings of ethics in at least the following ways:

1. They involve forms of moral agency that are diffuse and far-reaching, and that rarely involve direct rational choice.

2. It is very difficult or impossible to know the consequences of actions, values, and behaviors.

3. These problems involve entities, such as ecosystems or "dying cultures," that are not easily accommodated by ethics that value people, utility, sentient beings, or communities of people.

4. These problems involve past and future generations, and therefore the cultivation of a sense of responsibility on the part of people who are not directly responsible for postcolonial circumstances (although those people may contribute to them, in large and small ways).

5. Our practical and ethical options are severely limited, or overdetermined, by forces beyond our control, and so in most matters we seem forced to choose from among a set of relative evils.

What are the ethics of knowledge-production in *this* moral world? What is the philosophy that this world needs? What do we want to create with our labor? How can we, as knowledge producers, be in the business of getting closer, instead of farther away, from the world that forms our substance?

This argument is not meant to imply that we have solved our regular old moral problems, or that ethical knowledge was adequate until we became a high-tech global village. Work in feminist ethics has made evident how ethical theory has historically neglected some of the most fundamental aspects of human moral life. But the endlessly flawed twentieth-century moral imagination is woefully inadequate to address the intricate webs of relation created by global capitalism, postcolonial realities, and the fact that the environment has no borders. We are prosperous, preposterous moral beings with a litany of responsibilities that seem nearly impossible to know, let alone enact. The sense that one need be not only a saint, but also either insane or very rich in order to do the right thing is more evidence of the extent to which our ethical choices are overdetermined by corporations, profit-motivated scientific research, and free trade agreements that conspire against our making even simple moves in the right direction. The fact that doing the right thing too often seems tantamount to buying the right thing (solar panels, memberships in environmental organizations, locally-stitched organic cotton clothing) or not buying the wrong thing (grapes, plastic baby diapers, toxic underarm deodorant) is an indicator that there are some interesting and important questions in ethics for philosophers to work out in contexts that include public spaces.

I propose that we engage, or recommit ourselves, to the project of getting closer. The project of getting closer involves attempts to bridge knowledge and action by bringing thinkers, knowers, and actors closer to the worlds affected by our actions and inaction. This project requires research that brings us closer to nature and closer to each other, in a nonromantic, epistemic, and affective sense; that helps us know more about our interdependencies and that enables us to care for what we care about.

Philosophy is only one discourse that might assist us in determining what it means to be variously positioned, historically located moral agents, and how we might be responsible participants in a global economic community. Knowledge producers of all sorts can work to capture and address the real textures of our lives, to make it possible to live well without wreaking havoc on the world around us. For example, we might give more attention to the various factors that shape ethical efficacy, including how knowledge production in general is implicated in our failure to find the moral guidance and motivation that we so desperately need, and how scientific and technological projects which are beholden to private interests, or to a vision of progress that is killing us, manage to thrive in our universities.

One of the main obstacles to the knowledge projects that aim to get closer is an academic stance that begins with arrogance, and that bolsters the state-sponsored arrogance of economically privileged actors. Getting closer requires curiosity and caring across chasms of ontological and cultural difference. It requires openness to truths that are virtually unimaginable without the perspectives of those who are considered outsiders, and so can only be engaged with an awareness of its own partiality, and the fact that it is always incomplete. Knowledge projects that aim to get closer are aware of their own limits, and of the vulnerability of any knower, and of any knowledge.

Perhaps most naughtily, knowledge producers who aim to get closer abandon the dream of scientific progress that seeks absolute knowledge in the service of enlightened mastery and wealth, working instead for knowledge that gives us all a feeling for the organism (to use Barbara McClintock's phrase), that acquaints us with the particulars of the world we affect. Science and technology, in particular, can help us get closer by creating alternatives to our present habits.

Arrogant inquiries accept a comfortable distance between knowledge and life, and hide their limits and inadequacies behind an epistemic posture that proclaims a unified route to knowing, a route that necessarily follows academic traditions of privilege and exclusion.

If we want to get closer, it is easy to know that academic arrogance comes not only from a lack of humility, but also from a mistaken picture of our place in the world.

Lesbian and Its Synonyms (An Essay for All Feminists)

In this essay, I want "lesbian" to symbolize "lesbian and its syn-onyms"—a gendered homoerotic term. Of course "female homo-sexual," "bulldagger," "queer girl," "dyke," and their synonyms (add your own) reside in different and overlapping worlds, and carry distinct meanings and references. But they are also fairly translatable cultural equivalents. The contexts where they are not translatable are important and interesting, but that is not where I begin. I begin with an ontology of connection among what sensibly comes under the sign. This essay therefore imagines contexts in which lesbian is translatable—I can imagine these contexts because I have been there.

"Lesbian" is a category that names transgressive homoerotics, like the terms gay and queer, but lesbian and its synonyms marks these as female. "Lesbian" includes female agency and female subject/object relations. It is both a noun and an adjective.

What is a lesbian? A woman who prefers sex with women? A woman who is erotically inclined mostly toward other women?

Hard to say.

There are women who are not lesbians who occasionally or habitually enjoy (or long to enjoy) sex with other women. There are lesbians who are celibate, lesbians who enjoy sex with men, and lesbians who hate sex. Are women who are mostly attracted to women, but who are sexually involved mostly with men, really lesbians? Who decides what a lesbian is, and when and where it matters?

In the heyday of twentieth century lesbian feminism, a popular definition of *lesbian* was "woman-loving-woman." At the beginning of the twenty-first century, if you've spent any time on the borders of gender, such a definition seems too simple, if not naive. We can't really get a handle on "lesbian" without figuring out some things about gender and sex, but you know where we're going to end up with all that: categories like woman and sex have multiple meanings and are socially constituted, as are the bodies through which they are made real. Once you look closely at the concepts and realities involved, there seems no way the claim "a lesbian is a woman-loving-woman" could be true.

The issue is not just about abstract meanings. Changes in technology and social practices create tricky figures who shake up the very categories and boundaries that interest us, and that shape our interests. We know women who were born as male bodies, who do sex and romance with other women, including lesbians. We know men and boys who were once women themselves, or who were once lesbians, who are now male lovers of women. Does a full-blown male identity make the lesbian disappear? Does the possibility of male lesbians endanger the existence of lesbian women? Again, it depends. We know that bilateral sex distinction is a complex endeavor, not a biological dualism, but it is not always easy to incorporate that knowledge into clear language, understanding, or politics. And then there are the complications of sexuality.

At times our lives seem definable through categories of identity. When genders and body games are so influential in shaping human life and determining where one sits in relation to others, it seems to make sense to describe sexual identity in terms of gender and practice. But life is rarely as simple as the labels that determine partner benefits. I would guess that most hot-blooded humans are aroused watching Michael Jordan play basketball, or Madonna dance. Human movement through erotic landscapes is not reducible to what the conscious mind tells us, or even who our lovers are. The range of what drives us through the curves, scents, and swells of human intimacy cannot be captured by available woman/man/homo/hetero categories of identity. Sexuality is a realm of endless variety and particularity. Must it be something that provides an identity?

Power-laden and partial, terms of sexual identity are always complex, and always revised and contested. But lesbians seem uncommonly obsessed with brandishing, challenging, and ogling the term that names them. Looking at feminist scholarship and all sorts of queer cultures, we find that the conceptual borders of lesbian reality are defended and transgressed with unusual passion. Why is "lesbian" such a probed and contested category? Gay men would *never* worry that much about the meanings of "gay." Why do lesbians tend to make such a fuss?

Homophobic and misogynist norms say that lesbian differences are moral—whatever distinguishes lesbian is sinful or aberrant, and something that should not be encouraged. Liberal perceptions are that lesbian differences are neutral—that lesbian is a flavor of gay, which is in turn just a flavor of human desire. Feminist and queer theory aims to dispel negative readings of what distinguishes lesbians from others, but also to investigate how lesbian differences are politically relevant and positive—more than a natural species of human desire. In the eighties and nineties there was a flurry of groundbreaking work in philosophy that explored lesbian ethics as a uniquely illuminating moral position. The necessary political proximity of lesbian and feminism creates an unusually loaded identity, because such forbidden female agency criticizes the hierarchical order of gender, and therefore uniquely names a potentially feminist political category. "Lesbian" requires the idea that the female body is not a passive vessel. Theoretical engagement with lesbian meanings are so common, and so heated, because there is so much at stake.

The threat of violence against women and the identification of male bodies with patriarchal law (still) create feminist and lesbian desires for women-only space. The constitution of such spaces creates physical borders and provocative sites to be protected and transgressed. "Lesbian" is so highly contested because it is so loaded, but also because there are so many places where it *can* be dissected and defended. In addition to women-only zones (from music festivals to Internet chatrooms), there are thriving political groups, journals, Women's Studies programs, cafés and coffeehouses, bookstores and bars, cruises and workshops and parties. And anyone who has spent much time with lesbians knows they tend to be a fairly ponderous, protective, and opinionated bunch.

Lesbian and its synonyms indicate transgression of social law regarding proper female sexual personhood, in the context of a minimally mutual (female-female) transgression. Given the powerful sex-and-gender taboos against lesbian options, it is instructive to notice how they are made real in the world. How is mutual embodied female loving possible in a world that degrades female bodies and enforces strict laws against free homoerotic expression? How might we encourage such expression, or free and mutual erotic expression of any sort? Noticing lesbian difference, and the contours of meaning within and against which it exists, exposes fascinating truths about bodies, sex, and gender. Looking at patterns of resistance to misogyny and heteronormativity clarifies feminist and queer politics, and provides clues about the many-leveled political relevance of lesbians and other queer women. The variety of realities represented by *lesbian* and its synonyms also makes the terrain a compelling site for investigating politics of race and class (a fascinating example is Lisa Duggan's, *Sapphic Slashers: Sex, Violence, and American Modernity*). There are still good reasons why it is helpful to inquire about the meanings of *lesbian*.

What Does a Lesbian Look Like?

Feminist philosopher Cheshire Calhoun has suggested we investigate lesbian differences—what is distinct about lesbians—by looking how lesbians have been represented historically. In her essay "The Gender

Closet: Lesbian Disappearance under the Sign 'Women,' " Cheshire considers lesbian icons such as Rosa Bonheur, the Ladies of Llangollen, Gertrude Stein, Radclyffe Hall, and the white and black butch lesbians of the 1940s and 1950's (as described in books such as Davis and Kennedy's, *Boots of Leather, Slippers of Gold*) and finds that the figures who represent and symbolize lesbians, who make "lesbian" thinkable, are gender deviants. Calhoun argues that these notorious figures best represent the lesbian because they have the power to generate the question, "To what sex does she belong?"

The first thing to notice about such an analysis is how culture's biases create icons, and how history's biases present them. By taking representations at face value instead of investigating their relationships to various economies, Cheshire inherits a too-narrow cultural view. Still, it is true that many people identify the butches as the real lesbians:

> 'Golly, got on men's clothes and everything, what kind of women are these?' Then I started seeing more women here dressed in stone men's attire. I said, 'Well, golly, these are funny women.' Then they kind of fascinated me. What could they possibly do? Everybody wants to know what can you do. I got curious and I said, 'I'm going to find out.'
>
> ARLETTE, in *Boots of Leather, Slippers of Gold*

The view that gender ambiguity is central to the meaning of "lesbian" is persuasive, and it is an argument made from various cultural contexts. Nathalie Micas, Bonheur's womanly partner, doesn't do the trick, and neither does Alice B. Toklas. Those (femme) figures do not scream "lesbian," because they have too much in common with women. They *are* lesbians, of course, but from the perspective of theory, looking at them does not tell us much about what lesbians are, or what "lesbian" means. Cheshire's argument is that, "it is not same-sex desire, but an ambiguous relation to the categories 'woman' and 'man' that most powerfully represents the lesbian" (22). Her argument hinges on her belief that lesbian distance from gender norms explains feminism's failure to adequately address lesbian interests.

This view of lesbian difference is not unusual. It is a theme in feminist philosophy that deviation from the norms associated with gender and biological sex are fundamental to the meaning of lesbian. Women are made, not born, after all. Lesbian choices are resistances to the deep norms of womanhood, and therefore to the most fundamental categories of being. Lesbians create forms of being beyond the simple dualisms of sex and gender, and so enactments of new creations—visible performances of the woman who is not a woman—make lesbian possibilities real. This sort of analysis captures the depth of lesbian transgression of wide social norms, and it is responsive to the experience of the power of lesbian existence, found in positions outside the presumed logic of culture.

> *I am she who bellows with her three horns, I am the triple one, I am the formidable benevolent infernal one, I am the black the red and the white, I am the very great tall powerful one she whose noxious breath has poisoned thousands of generations so be it.*
>
> MONIQUE WITTIG, *The Lesbian Body*

The tale of the lesbian rising into the power of consciousness, her armor cast from rejections of femininity, her intelligence as certain as her separateness from men, is a familiar one. But though she emphasizes her own heroics, this body is always both singular and *relational*. Lesbian requires mutual otherness that provides both meeting place with the other and challenge to self, because "lesbian" is inherently erotic. Approaches that focus on gender to the exclusion of sexuality conceive "lesbian" as a form of individual being—an identity, not a relation. It is true that lesbians are not women, or not-quite women, and that the energy of lesbian existence is generated by the tension between lesbian rejection of and love for what is implied by Woman, and our multiple positions as outside/insiders to those games. And lesbian erotic connection occurs, however ambiguously, through and against woman as embodied subject (lover) and object (lovee).

When we look for the lesbian in cultural representation, we are bound to find a singular character possessing an outlaw sexuality that seems to dwell within, and an outlaw identity that presents itself through public (chaste and external) signs. Only recently, or only in very select contexts, has lesbian sexuality itself been displayed. The ease with which the mannish lesbian has historically symbolized the lesbian to the world says more about the politics of representation in heterosexual economies and institutions than it does about lesbian differences. Female inverts like Radclyffe Hall most effectively symbolized female homoerotic options for sexologists who were looking for lesbian deformity directly on the body. The transgressions of gender that made working-class black butches visible as bulldykes in 1950s Buffalo were also culturally specific, and read in light of specific politics of representation. It is not irrelevant that butch lesbians more seamlessly or effectively represent lesbian differences, and not surprising that symbolically powerful tomboys make lesbians identifiable to straight audiences. There is no more reliable creator of notoriety than enactments of the wrong sex, and culture focuses on the most visible lesbians. But to whom is culture speaking? How much can cultural representation tell us about lesbian differences? When we look at lesbians, the complications of relationality, resistance, and representation make anything as simple as "the lesbian" disappear.

One motivation for a theoretical emphasis on individual gender nonconformity rather than sex is the fact that so much homophobia is directed against visible nonconformity, and so it seems that what is most significant about queerness is its challenges to gender norms. Many lesbians and gay men with economic privilege would say they experience the direct ill-will of others' homophobia more commonly in relation to employment, housing, partner benefits, marriage, and adoption (areas of life that can be legislated), and less in relation to our sex lives. In democratic contexts, people are more likely to articulate and enforce the law "Marriage should be between a woman and a man," not "Queer sex should be prohibited." Even wingnut conservative preachers can seem more concerned with our domestic lives than they are with our sex lives (I've sometimes wondered if conservatives are faking it when they seem *so* freaked out by queer sex, given how many of them seem to enjoy unconventional sex lives). Listening to their public rhetoric, it's easy to believe that homophobic conservatives are most concerned about the lesbian and gay threat to the traditional family. Isn't that why they hate feminists too?

We should not take the family values hype at face value. Sex panic is deeply interwoven with conservative worries about sex-and-gender norms. It is what lesbians represent about sex, gender, and power that makes homophobic people so uncomfortable. Taboos against sexual freedoms and practices are enforced through shame, and through legislation requiring gender conformity. The fact that wingnuts are always blaming feminists and lesbians and gays for the decay of the traditional family is an indication that there is something about unfettered female existence and unfettered sexuality that is perceived as unusually powerful.

Cheshire's questions about representation fail to pay attention to lesbian bodies. Oddly, sex and erotic relationality drop out of her notion of "lesbian" because it is the confused observer—the straight world, and not the lesbian gaze—that directs her to the lesbians. Lesbian difference is not merely a matter of gender deviance, appearance, or representation. It is a matter of all these in relation to sexuality and embodied desire.

What Do Lesbians Do?

Sex was happily rolling around with boys who had learned about my body from other little boys and dirty magazines. Sex was an exchange of favors in a pretend-zone of complete freedom. I'm older now than my mother was then and still I am a body shaped in part by the lessons learned at the hands of fairly nice little boys (I was lucky) whose map of my body was provided by their big brothers, and magazines.

You will be cool if you do this. People will make fun of you if you do that. It feels great, but you have to do it in private. It is dirty or sinful or gross. It has everything to do with your self-esteem.

I do not want that story in this essay about lesbians but it seems crucial for remembering that the body is not a given, and that mutilating power can sneak into deceptively innocent interactions.

There are no analytic claims that can be made about lesbians, or lesbian behaviors or desires. Every sexuality references a body that is open to interpretation. Every sexuality has its own dynamic language games, fantasies, memories, aspirations, and chemistries. A sexual identity is a pattern that takes the name of the category that best suits it, if it must take a name at all. When sexuality is contiguous with normalcy, it needs no name—its name is "human." When the association of a particular sexuality with normalcy has been exposed as a power-laden lie and a form of social control, every sexual self-in-process becomes a matter of interpretation.

Since sex is such a secret, there not many witnesses who can tell us what we are, and so the shamefulness of sex provides the luxury of describing our own patterns. Patterns in the form of girlfriends-or-boyfriends seems to make the straight/gay/bi distinction obvious. Or patterns of preference can be your own little secret, if you care to notice them at all. But how does one describe the *energy* of life's desire, the way it moves and changes, demands and peaks? The mutuality that makes it worth naming?

Sexuality is a form of bodily modification. Sexuality is connected to the energetic core of human existence and happiness. There is no body zone that is *the* erotic zone, but genitals are special. They are moist, distracting, engagingly erectile, exceedingly sensitive, and hormonally responsive. As a region of erotic love, the pelvis is paradigmatic and popular. The human body evolved for connection and pleasure, sex and love (among other things).

Any naturalized conception of sexuality is a fictional account. Some philosophers have played with the idea that lesbians don't really have sex, because sex is a heteropatriarchal practice that depends on and reifies the centrality of the phallus and male domination. The arguments were politically interesting and provocative, but since lesbian sex has quite a lot in common with other sex, they ultimately didn't catch on.

The only way to gain additional CHI is to transform sexual energy that would normally be released in lovemaking by recycling it back into CHI, thereby providing us with an extra 30 to 40 percent of life-force. In this book you will learn the Taoist methods of Healing Love to accomplish this: namely, Ovarian Breathing and the Orgasmic Upward Draw.

MANTAK CHI AND MANEEWAN CHIA,
Healing Love through the Tao: Cultivating Female Sexual Energy

Lesbian is a sexual identity, or *way*, that uniquely references femaleness. But what is a female body? It is impossible to extract the body's potential from the millennia of influences that have formed it. Does the sexual body consist of seven chakras, twelve meridians, five elements, nine systems, four bases, or one essential truth? What is a female sexual body who refuses the reproductive imagination?

She stretched, bent over, flexed and extended her muscles, and felt everything zing open. Different stretches, different openings. But her lower back was still tight, locked into something. She sat directly on the floor and stretched up and forward—bending from her hips bones flat against the carpet, and focusing on that whole region of the lower back that is so tight and protected all the time. Let it stretch, and came up to a less intense stretch so she could feel the region comfortably. And then from there she folded out and over again, felt the sacrum open up and fill, and even now as she relaxed, she felt a tingling and heat and aliveness that was quite distinct, erotic, even though it did not pulse toward the front of her body. A flash of knowledge: My back is not the back of me. It is fully me, just as relevant and real as the rest of me, as my face and biceps and breasts.

The fact is that people walk without any clear understanding of the guiding and controlling orders which command the satisfactory co-ordination and adjustment of the psycho-physical mechanism in the act of walking. . . . Re-education on a general basis . . . will restore satisfactory functioning throughout the organism, and so ensure a continued raising of the standard of psycho-physical equilibrium right on through life.

F. MATTHIAS ALEXANDER, *The Alexander Technique*

Although most medical textbooks still label the glans as "the clitoris," the actual clitoris is far more extensive. In 1981 the Federation of Feminist Women's Health Centers redefined the clitoris in its book, *A New View of Women's Body*, as a structure that includes not only the hood and glans but also a shaft, legs, muscles, and bulbs. In 1998 an Australian urologist, Helen O' Connell, described the glans as attached to a shaft of pyramid-shaped erectile tissue about the size of the first joint of the thumb... She also described the many nerves, blood vessels, and smooth muscles of the clitoris, which is made of the same erectile tissue as the penis and which swells during arousal.

To find the body of the clitoris, which together with the glans is two to four centimeters long, you need to feel directly behind the glans to the shaft, which feels like a firm, movable cord right under the skin. Attached to the shaft are the two clitoral legs that you can't see or feel at all. The legs, or crura, are nine to eleven centimeters long, and flare backward into the body, spreading out like a wide wishbone; they attach to the inferior aspect of the pubic bone. The clitoral bulbs—usually called the bulbs of the vestibule and rarely recognized in medical textbooks as part of the clitoris—are two bundles of erectile tissue that extend down the sides of the vestibule, the area just outside the vagina, and surround the urethra. The vestibular bulbs are connected to the glans of the clitoris.

During sexual arousal, the bulbs, legs, shaft, and glans of the clitoris become firm and filled with blood. The legs and the bulbs are both surrounded by muscle tissue (the bulbocavernosus and ischiocavernosus muscles), which, when contracted, help to create tension during arousal and the spasms felt during orgasm.

JENNIFER BERMAN AND LAURA BERMAN, *For Women Only: A Revolutionary Guide to Overcoming Sexual Dysfunction and Reclaiming Your Sex Life*

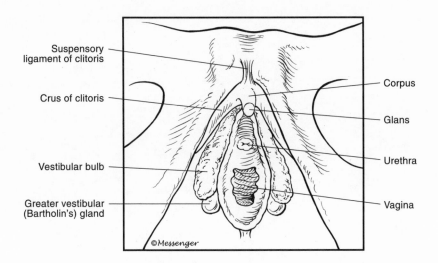

Suspensory ligament of clitoris

Crus of clitoris

Vestibular bulb

Greater vestibular (Bartholin's) gland

Corpus

Glans

Urethra

Vagina

©Messenger

Sometimes it is a workout. Sometimes a conversation, sometimes a trance. A comedy, a drama. Sometimes a struggle. There is she on this side and the other as well. Of course, there could be many.

A friend gave me a wall hanging from India featuring an image she takes to be lesbian. The scene is of two women in saris churning butter, mirror forms facing one another. It evokes the intimacy of a world of action and exchange. A world that transgresses the same logic that circumscribes it. (When the newspapers in India discuss lesbians, they tend to mention Ellen or Martina and the butter churners are nowhere in sight. Though I'm told things are better since the film *Fire* caused such a ruckus.) It is wonderful and tragic to feel as though you must find your own way.

We know we are not bound by what others have been able to imagine, yet we feel the absence of role models and useful information. Coming-out literatures and comparisons between lesbian and other female sexualities give the impression that a lesbian is about what she does not do. For animals who are capable of interacting erotically with just about anything in the world, any sexuality is a narrowing-down that involves both yes-saying and no-saying. What are the varieties of lesbian yes-saying? Should we assume it is something only lesbians do?

As the body shifts, gender shifts in the body. I know many women who love dressing like boys, but they've found it harder to find boy-style clothes for older women's bodies, and with wrinkles and duller hair, they feel they look better with a little makeup on. Unpredictable transformations ripple out into gender and sexuality. Age, culture, technology, desire. . . . As cultures shift, fantasy shifts as well. Back in the fifties or the seventies did anyone foresee the current lesbian baby boom? Are all of those lesbian mommies having sex? How does queer parenting shift and inform sexual realities?

History shapes fascinating lesbian worlds. What patterns and possibilities find their way into discourse and become influential, and why?

Have you heard the joke about lesbian bed death? It's a stereotype that after a few years of hot passionate sex, things cool off dramatically for lesbians. Long-term couples settle into and for relationships that feature more cuddling than sex. Funny, huh? I assumed that if it is true that lesbians have less sex than hets and fags (that's what the surveys say, so it must be true), it was because of the lack of testosterone. I theorized that the chemically invigorated male sex drive was a reliable somatic force that kept straight and gay male couples more sexually active. Without that extra initiating factor (not to mention the dangling ever-ready erectile tissue), I thought maybe it's too easy for lesbians to get lazy about maintaining good sexual connections with longtime lovers, even when they want them.

Then Viagra was born, letting us all know that STRAIGHT BED DEATH is a problem as well, and the testosteronic body is not as reliably responsive as it was rumored to be (except perhaps for gay men, but that's a different essay). Who knew straight men were having such a hard time getting it up? *Who indeed?* Another patriarchal lie shattered, another simple truth with fascinating implications. What is there to be learned from the Viagra phenomenon about aging and masculinity, bodies and desire? What use is made of the new awareness that so many men have been suffering from limpness?

Who knows. Who cares?

They diagnose a dysfunction, reduce it to a problem of chemistry, and then medicate.

There are reasons to be grateful for science's ignorance of lesbians.

A simple equation never captures a truth that is the only thing we need to know about what it describes.

> *Sky Woman had a peculiar trait: she had curiosity. She bothered the others with her questions, with wanting to know what lay beneath the clouds that supported her world. Sometimes she pushed the clouds aside and looked down through her world to the large expanse of blue that shimmered below. The others were tired of her peculiar trait and called her an aberration, a queer woman who asked questions, a woman who wasn't satisfied with what she had.*
>
> BETH BRANT (Degonwadonti), " This Is History"

Kaza turns thirty, gorgeous as a flower in full bloom in the stretchy minidress I bought her in Venice Beach. A heavy chunk of pearl rests at the base of her neck, knotted on a sinew of leather. Her huge eyes are sparkling blue, and her crazy curls are pulled back with a t-shirt sleeve that she's converted into a headwrap. A fashion trick learned on the ultimate frisbee team.

It's unseasonably chilly at the outdoor bar, but she bares her shoulders, slides her sweater off so I can touch her skin, and so she can enjoy my watching her. I was hating my body today and getting dressed for dinner made me a crabby bitch. Her sweet gaze and a glass of wine helps, and I pledge never to be an asshole again.

This is how we grow older together, two women in love. We are not wives. We witness each other with insider knowledge and distance. Crusaders sometimes, we have enough money to enjoy, to be aware, to go wild. We feel lucky beyond words, beyond what anyone should be able to enjoy in such a wicked world. We have a tribe, and many cultures. When we are not among them—most of the time—we live at the edges of wherever we are. We work hard and listen to every kind of music. We are true lovers of fun.

A friend of hers once reflected on how wonderful it was to love and be loved. 'I don't know what you're talking about,' Joe said. 'I don't love people.' Some of this was bravado. Joe's girlfriends remembered her as extremely affectionate and romantic. . . . But she did her best to dispense with feelings of love or pain . . . (writing) Love is just a phase, / To laugh, / and turn your face/ Away from time!

KATE SUMMERSCALE,
The Queen of Whale Cay

The girl Debbie stands sweating and smoking cigarettes in the urine fog of the subway. How would it be to have a girl like Debbie's arteries dilate around you in a slow red rush of velvet drapes? How would it feel to tune Debbie's body into a swollen receptacle made of hot corpuscles like a wet fleshy bed where you could screamingly discharge your rage and fear and then relax? I'm a girl but I pretend I'm a guy pushing in and out of you. . . . Girls

never end and that's their beauty; shoot one down and an even younger one
pops up in her place.

LAURIE WEEKS, " Debbie's Barium Swallow"

A world war going on
but you and I still insisting
in each our own heads
still thinkin how
if I could only make some contact
with that woman across the keyboard
we size each other up
yes. . .

CHERRÍE MORAGA, *Loving in the War Years*

"Woman"-"loving"-"woman"

There is no such thing as *the* lesbian perspective, but the politics of sexuality create patterns of engagement. I want a conception of sexual
identity that is loose and evocative enough to be useful, and that accurately sketches my tribe.

Sexuality is a form of bodily modification. The body that will not
ignore desire, the body who wants it badly enough, cannot help but tell
the truth. Queers display the ridiculousness of sexual laws, and the vulnerability of the heart. Lesbians also expose some of the lies of patriarchal culture.

All queers are truth tellers about sexuality, and that is what makes
us so threatening to maintainers of the gendered (raced and classed)
status quo. (Of course this does not mean that queers are particularly
honest.) By making forbidden homoerotics visible in cultures that asso-
ciate sex with shame and love, queers become cultural representatives
of both sexual freedom and the power of love. "Coming out" is portrayed as taking a dramatic stand for love, especially when it involves
the announcement of a legitimate partnership. The love that dare not
speak its name—we shout its name! The intensity of this proclamation

is obvious at gay weddings. For lesbians and gay men, weddings are dramatic displays of loving someone enough to declare it publicly in a world that severely punishes such pronouncements. Queers suffer for love (or so the fantasy goes), and so we make the power of love visible. Because we seem willing to make the shameful visible because of love, we are symbolically aligned with ethics of caring that value love and connection over rule-following and calculating reason. In testifying to the power of love, all queers are therefore identified with the despised feminine.

Queers also suffer for sex (another fantasy), and so we make visible the power of the sexual body. We are willing to make the shameful visible because of desire, so we are symbolically aligned with ethics of eros that value physical pleasure, touch, and experience over rule-following and calculating reason. In testifying to the power of desire, queers represent the despised body.

Our truth-telling about the absurdities of sex and gender is one thing that makes queers such a funny and clever bunch.

And what about the lesbians? In 1982, Marilyn Frye described gendered reality as something like a play in which men are the actors—the ones to whom we're supposed to pay attention—and women are the stagehands. She argued that accepting the sexist politics of reality requires keeping one's attention focused on the actors and ignoring the stagehands. Of course, if you fix your attention on the women in the background, and not on the men, you see that what is supposed to be reality is just a performance, and you also see all the work women do to keep the show running. Lesbians have a unique epistemic location, Frye argued (back in the day when it seemed like a good idea to link identity and labour directly to epistemic privilege) because lesbians see the women.

Nowadays we see the limits of Frye's one-dimensional gender analysis. Even if the majority are women, the gruntworkers of reality are not just women, and their social position is more often determined by class and race than by gender. And of course many women are fully visible and influential as actors. Still, there is something

about the image of *seeing the women* that does capture a lesbian incli-
nation. "Seeing" the "women" (and *wanting to be seen* by "them") is
evident in the mutuality and identity in the meanings of lesbian. It is
even evident in characters like postlesbian boys and bisexual women,
whose presence may be seen as a call for a radical deconstruction of
lesbian meanings.

Bisexual former-lesbians struggle to find names for who they have
become, as do transgendered folks negotiating simultaneous shifts in
gender and sexuality. Interestingly, formerly lesbian bisexuals tend to
describe something in their perspectives or consciousness that remains
sufficiently similar to "the way they were before" to still be lesbian, or
lesbian*ish*. Pat Califia, a former lesbian who is now a gay man (and
whose male partner is also a former lesbian) describes himself as still
quite a lot like a lesbian, because women remain the center of his
focus. "A bisexual is saying 'men and women are of equal importance.'
That's simply not true of me" (185). In Kristin Esterberg's book about
lesbian and bisexual identities, the theme of perspective emerges over
and over again. As one former lesbian says, "There is a certain way you
think, there's a certain way you look at things. . . . Just because you're
involved in a different sexual behavior doesn't mean you lose that
whole consciousness" (67, and discussed in Bachmann).

When we look at the testimony and descriptions offered by the
wide range of players in the lesbian family, we end up with a conception of "lesbian" that is surprisingly close to what we began with as an
outdated cliché. If "woman" is taken to be a multiplicitous and shifting
social category, not a natural one, and "loving" is taken to indicate
erotic engagement (as vague and wide-ranging as sexuality always is),
then perhaps a lesbian is a "woman"-"loving"-"woman," and lesbian
things (fantasies, experiences, and experiments) are imbued with that
way. "Woman"-"loving"-"woman" is a family resemblance, not an analytic concept.

For a "woman," seeing the women or seeing the lesbians includes
seeing oneself in illuminating ways. Whatever a woman is, if you're a
woman (if there is a "woman" in there somewhere), once you see the

women, once you include women in your erotic or sexual universe, it can't be easy to go back to not seeing them, even if you become a lover of men, even if you don't identify as one of the women anymore. Once you have experienced that form of attention, why would you want to go back?

Lesbians do have special knowledge. Lesbians are truth-tellers about female bodies, and they signify the fact that women rule. Not that women ought to rule, but that women *do* rule—they have desire, enact knowledge, and take command. They even choose to not be women. It is worth suffering to love them.

Anyone who knows that women rule (that women are full persons and that women are fully lovable), and who sees that women do not rule, is bound to be disappointed with the world. Lesbians are natural discontents. They are critics of the order of things. They claim the right to be full human beings, and the fact that they have a thing for women weaves a pattern of compassion among their tribe. They are uppity people who defend the feminine by freeing it from the spell of femininity. They have a tough softness that can be off-putting or beguiling. They are certainly useful in difficult situations.

Reading Simone Weil: It's Better to Fade Away

After the bombing of New York I was seeking philosophical guidance. I was worried about where we were headed, and I had no confidence in political leaders. I wasn't looking for analysis—I had analyses that satisfied me. I was plagued by questions, and looking for insight and inspiration.

One night I was in the mood to read the reflections of a writer who'd lived under fascism, but I could not find Hannah Arendt on the bookshelf of my Brooklyn apartment. Luckily, just a couple of weeks earlier, I'd been given a book by Simone Weil.

The French philosopher Simone Weil (1909–1934) lived a short, intense, sad, and ecstatic life. Weil is perhaps best known for her mystical writing, but she was also a brilliant political thinker, a sharp critic of blind patriotism, and an innovator of practical philosophy. Like reading Nietsche for the first time, reading Simone Weil can be a delightful and annoying trip. I was initially drawn in by her incisive aphoristic offerings:

> The question of the best means to employ to prevent a conspiracy from aris-
> ing in high places with the object of obtaining immunity from the law is
> one of the most difficult political problems to solve. It can only be solved if

there are men whose duty it is to prevent such a conspiracy, and whose sit-
uation in life is such that they are not tempted to enter into it themselves
(The Need for Roots, 22).

Fear and terror, as permanent states of the soul, are wellnigh mortal poi-
sons, whether they be caused by the threat of unemployment, police perse-
cution, the presence of a foreign conqueror, the probability of invasion, or
any other calamity which seems too much for human strength to bear. . . .
Even if permanent fear constitutes a latent state only, so that its painful
effects are only rarely experienced directly, it remains always a disease. It is
a semi-paralysis of the soul (The Need for Roots, 33).

Weil's politics were deeply spiritual. Her philosophical work was
guided by a desire to respond appropriately to a world of suffering, and
her life was an attempt to move theory into practice. In her characteristically melodramatic and masochistic explorations of the love of God,
her belief that suffering is both inevitable and beneficial is apparent:

It is in affliction itself that the splendor of God's mercy shines, from its
very depths, in the heart of its inconsolable bitterness. If still persevering
in our love, we fall to the point where the soul cannot keep back the cry,
"My God, why hast thou forsaken me?" if we remain at this point without
ceasing to love, we end by touching something that is not affliction, not joy,
something that is the central essence, necessary and pure, something not of
the senses, common to joy and sorrow: the very love of God (Waiting for
God, 89).

Simone Weil's parents both came from observant Jewish families,
though they raised Simone and her brother in an atheist and assimilated home. Weil completely rejected her Jewish identity—one biogra-
pher describes her as a "self-exiled Jew," and her strange anti-Semitic
bias is a recurrent theme in the vast literature on her work. Although
she was passionately attached to Roman Catholicism, Weil refused to
be baptized. She believed such a commitment to a worldly institution

would conflict with her primary responsibility, which was to be as critical and probing as possible in her quest for the truth. Her dedication to philosophy was profound, yet Simone believed "manipulators of words, whether priests or intellectuals, have always been on the side of the ruling class, on the side of the exploiters against the producers" (in McLellan, 47). Clearly she wanted to be different.

Supported by an upper-class family, Simone nonetheless identified with the oppressed, declaring herself a Bolshevik at age ten and choosing throughout her life to reject privilege and simulate working- class existence. These commitments were not merely symbolic. Simone de Beauvoir, her contemporary, wrote that she envied Weil "for having a heart that could beat right across the world." Weil participated in revolutionary workers' movements, wrote political pamphlets and essays, and taught philosophy and classics to factory workers. Before the war broke out she spent time in Germany observing the everyday realities of life under Nazism, and she joined the effort at the front during the Spanish Civil War.

Anticipating a wealth of contemporary work in feminist ethics, in *The Need for Roots* Weil argued that rights do not capture the depth of what is valuable about human life and experience. She believed the self who can be crushed by oppression or lifted by spirituality is not a holder of rights but a soul with needs. She wrote, "Thanks to this word [rights], what should have been a cry of protest from the heart has been turned into a shrill nagging of claims and counter-claims, which is both impure and impractical" ("Human Personality," in Miles, 64). Justice is not merely a matter of addressing inequality—it demands a response to the question "Why am I being hurt?" To serve human well-being, social life therefore should be guided not by rights, but by relation of respect, care, and obligation.

Because Weil understood philosophical questions to be thoroughly practical, demanding bodily investigation and action, her life was a fascinating experiment in spiritual and political praxis. Her passionate engagement with life (and death) provides an unusually helpful illustration of the strengths and weaknesses of her philosophical positions.

Weil's insightful critique of Marx, for example, emerged from her experiences as a laborer. In 1934 Weil took a year's leave from a position teaching philosophy at a girls' school to realize a long-standing dream of testing Marx's theories by actually becoming a factory worker. Her health was always poor, but she sought out particularly difficult and demanding work. Simone's notebooks and letters from that period include scrupulous descriptions and analyses of grueling conditions:

> *The fire comes from five or six openings at the bottom of the furnace. I stand right in front of it to insert about thirty large metal bobbins. . . . I have to take great care that they fall into the open holes, because they would melt. Therefore I must stand close up to the furnace and not make any clumsy movement, in spite of the scorching heat on my face and the fire on my own arms (which still show the burns) (Miles, 14).*

Working in the factory led Simone to see fundamental flaws in Marx's analysis of oppression.

A primary theme of Weil's critique of Marxism (most fully articulated in the posthumously published essay "Reflections Concerning the Causes of Liberty and Social Oppression") is the fact that oppression is not a function of any particular form of production. It was evident to Weil that a general respect for justice could have easily prevented the wretched suffering she experienced and witnessed in the factory. Why, then, doesn't it? "Why," she asked, "should the division of labour necessarily turn into oppression?" (129). Echoing Nietzsche and anticipating Foucault, she believed the answer was to be found in an analysis of power; "Inequality would not lead to a still harsher form of necessity than that of natural needs themselves, were it not for the intervention of a further factor, namely, the struggle for power" (137).

The suffering of workers was horrible, but it was not unique. Suffering in the factory was like all human suffering, because like all suffering it originates in the exercise of oppressive force. Suffering therefore discloses truths about human agency and power, not just about capitalism. Marx failed to ask why exploitation nearly always and everywhere wins out over justice, and so he mistakenly thought that the problem was one particularly brutal system. But in every system the powerful treat the powerless like objects, and so it is actually people who create oppression. Weil defined oppression as the humiliation of being treated like an object and knowing that no other alternative exists. The above letter continues,

> *Working in a factory . . . meant that all the external reasons (which I had previously thought internal) upon which my sense of personal dignity, my self-respect, was based were radically destroyed within two or three weeks by the daily experience of brutal constraint. And don't imagine that this provoked in me any rebellious reaction. No, on the contrary; it produced the last thing I expected from myself—docility. The resigned docility of a beast of burden. It seems to me that I was born to wait for, and receive, and carry out orders—that I had never done and never would do anything else. . . . It is the kind of suffering no worker talks about: it is too painful even to think of it. . . . Slowly and painfully, in and through slavery. I reconquered the sense of my human dignity. . . . Accompanied always by the knowledge that I possessed no right to anything, and that any moment free from humiliation and suffering should be accepted as a favour, as merely a lucky chance.*
>
> *In all this I am speaking of unskilled work, of course (and especially the women's work).*
>
> *And in the midst of it all a smile, a word of kindness, a moment of human contact, have more value than the most devoted friendships among the privileged, both great and small. It is only there that one knows what human brotherhood is. But there is little of it, very little (15).*

The intolerable pit of suffering is the sense that one was born to carry out orders, and that one will never be anything else. The slavery of capitalism is a paradigm for all interactions where power is used to keep the subjugated in her place, and like all oppression it can be maintained only through intimidation and desperation. But oppression is ubiquitous, and Weil believed it is easy to see that its overall effects are not reduced with apparently revolutionary changes in a particular system of production. Wherever subordinates are regarded as objects, exploitation distorts agency and makes real revolutionary change impossible. Marx was overly optimistic about revolution because he did not understand the deep emotional dimensions of injustice or the pervasive and lasting effects of suffering, but Weil experienced these effects directly. She described how for a slave the very idea of time becomes unbearable and life becomes the anticipation of pain. In addition, a slave does not feel she has any rights, because rights dissolve when they are recognized by no one. So oppression is near-complete disempowerment, as described in the letter above.

Simone Weil's experiences and experiments convinced her that suffering was fundamental to the human condition. For philosophy to address such a foundational moral and political problem, it should not look for or dissect a particularly oppressive system. Sounding much like a contemporary feminist, Weil believed instead that the problem is to understand the common thread in all forms of oppression, "to know what it is that links oppression in general and each form of oppression in particular to the system of production, to grasp the mechanism of oppression, by what means it arises, subsists, transforms itself, and by what means, perhaps, it might theoretically disappear" (128).

Weil also addressed the question she believed Marx had ignored to the detriment of his entire philosophical and political project: *why* does oppression occur? Taking universal suffering as her starting point, she theorized a unified and universal cause to explain the effect. In her famous essay "*The Iliad*, or The Poem of Force," she describes the *Iliad* (one of her favorite works) as an illustration of "that *x* that turns anybody who is subjected to it into a thing" (163). That "x" is power, or force. It is exercised through action, enslaves through interaction, and can completely modify the human spirit. Through force, one man's power of presence turns another man into an object. "The master produces fear in the slave by the very fact that he is afraid of him, and vice versa; and the same is true as between rival powers" (138). In "Reflections Concerning the Causes of Liberty and Social Oppression" she describes force as a natural and material necessity. Human force is a displaced and phantom version of the force of nature, within which we must struggle to survive. Natural force turns nearly all human relations into oppressive ones and that causes suffering everywhere.

Thus far the analysis is strictly political. It is a story about the workings of power in the material and social world, and its devastating effects in contexts that are almost always shaped by stark inequalities. These contexts are the inheritance of endless histories formed through inevitable compliance with force, and so resistance to them is just about impossible. Weil does see one way out, but it requires both radical acceptance of suffering, and God.

Weil believed that only superhuman virtue or divine grace can provide the strength to refuse to exercise force over another, and that "the enlightened goodwill of men acting in an individual capacity is the only possible principle of social progress" (132). Because force is a natural necessity, we cannot escape it. But unless we are content to wield force over others (to be oppressors), we are born to carry out orders. To refuse to be an oppressor therefore requires taking on suffering oneself, and for slaves, meaningful life requires acceptance of inevitable suffering. The only act of freedom available is to choose to surrender to suffering. We cannot choose to reject suffering, but we can choose our master. That is, we can choose to say yes to suffering *because* it is the necessary condition presented by God. Accepting existence, accepting God, is accepting the duty to suffer. This is Weil's leap of faith, and in her view, the only way to transform and transcend inevitability.

In response to a world fashioned from oppression, virtue requires the personal acceptance of affliction, and consent to a world of suffering, "The only way into truth is through one's own annihilation, through dwelling in a state of extreme and total humiliation" ("Human Personality," 70). Loving existence (loving God) requires loving reality from the condition of suffering. And suffering is real, not symbolic, so the surrender must be physical. Disloyalty to force requires abandoning the illusions that impel us to negative force—illusions of the autonomous self, and illusions of control. Accepting suffering is tantamount to becoming a slave. Weil famously wrote, "Christianity is preeminently the religion of slaves, slaves cannot help belonging to it, and I among others" (17). The slave is ecstatic in her knowledge of oneness with all of reality in suffering, where one finds "the love of God."

> In the heart of its inconsolable bitterness. . . . if we remain at this point without ceasing to love, we end by touching . . . the central essence, necessary and pure . . . the very love of God.

For Weil, therefore, ethical agency in the face of widescale human suffering requires the immolation of the very organism it hopes to set free.

How thoroughly Simone Weil trusted her perceptions of her own reality and the reality of others. Simone was always rather physically unwell, and it is clear that her personality was inherently attentive to suffering. Her intelligence looked suffering straight in the eye, and took responsibility for it. At the same time, she was a misfit and an outsider, and she had difficulty connecting deeply to other people. Unlike Beauvoir and Arendt, Weil never had a lover. Other than a few priests and admirers who considered her a not-of-the-world, saintly figure, she had few close friends. Even politically, Simone lacked a community that was not reducible to connection through co-enslavement. In her political organizing, comrades apparently regarded her as an outsider, and her creative response to suffering was a solo work.

Yet Weil understood her own suffering to be equivalent to the suffering of all slaves. She identified its salient features (becoming an object, anticipating only harm and pain) as foundational to the logic of power, and saw no earthly escape. Instead of raising interesting questions about survival (How do we survive suffering? How have others survived?), and about the differences between slavery as a consequence of identity and slavery as a chosen path, she found comfort in transcendence. Interestingly, her transcendent view was embodied—the way to salvation lay in acceptance of bodily realities, and in dutiful bodily practices. But her conception of what the body is is dualistic and earth-denying, because the earthly body is only a pathway to the ultimate reality, which is godly and not of the material world. Gravity drags us down, but full acceptance of the wretched suffering body brings spiritual grace, which is the only thing that can lift one from the body, and from one's prescribed role in an unjust world.

In *Philosophia*, Andrea Nye's compelling study of Weil, Rosa Luxemburg, and Hannah Arendt, Nye stresses Weil's materialism, and her embodied epistemology. Though this materialism is evident in her political theorizing and her praxis of embodied knowing, her ethics and spirituality are ultimately disturbingly disembodied. They are also highly individualistic. Her stark moral individualism is evident in her conception of redemptive virtue, and in her belief that "association is not a need, but an expedient employed in the practical affairs of life" (*The Need for Roots*, 22). Dismissive of collectivities, in *Gravity and Grace* she writes, "The vegetative and the social are the two realms where the good does not enter. . . . The social order is irreducibly that of the prince of this world. Our only duty with regard to the social is to try to limit the evil of it" (145). In addition, Weil's Platonic transcendentalism bolstered her belief that salvation lies in resistance to gravity and the down-drag of the material world, including other particular people:

> We have to be catholic, that is to say, not bound by so much as a thread to any created thing, unless it be to creation in its totality. . . . It is true that we have to love our neighbor, but, in the example that Christ gave as an illustration of this commandment, the neighbor is a being of whom nothing is known, lying naked, bleeding, and unconscious on the road. It is a question of completely anonymous, and for that reason, completely universal love (*Waiting for God*, 98).

Weil puts her trust in individual agency, yet the individual is no ethical goal:

> We possess nothing in the world—a mere chance can strip us of everyhing—except the power to say 'I'. That is what we have to give God—in other words, to destroy (*Gravity and Grace*, 23).

For Weil, agency begins with I, but it does not end there, because the I is a body that must be denied. Her ethics and metaphysics depend on the body falling away from her image of the true self. She was also a somatophobe who was paranoid about germs and did not like to hug or touch others because she feared her "disgustingness" might rub off on them. Like many earnest young women predisposed to hating their bodies, Simone considered the wretched body to be the site of intense suffering and the obstacle to goodness, yet she saw the power of the body as a means to achieving her own chosen ends. Love is a route to freedom, but the love that can free the body from suffering is transcendent, not embodied. Love requires submission to supernatural grace, "annihilation in (a) god who confers the fullness of being upon the creature so annihilated" (McLellan, 200). Like Platonic knowledge, grace does not require loving attention to the earthly body—it is found in the dazzling light above. Its realization is the experience of egoless serenity, not joy, for joy requires one who feels, and "in the soul filled by grace no corner is left for saying I" (*Gravity and Grace*, 27). The state of grace therefore bears a striking resemblance to death.

Poor Simone's brilliant critique of Marx, her political commitments, and her philosophical solutions to the problem of suffering did not seem to bring much benefit on the personal front, although her religious writing buzzes with obsessive beatific ecstasy. Knowledge of the fact that so many people are made or allowed to suffer so miserably, while others enjoy such relative comfort, was too much for Simone to bear. Having experienced the reality of suffering so dramatically and so deeply, Simone found that her only escape from painful knowledge came when she was engaged in difficult physical labour or contemplating God's love. The link she perceived between suffering in the world and the moral imperative of bodily denial was absolute. She relished physical discomfort because it distracted her and assured her that she was doing the right thing.

As paradigmatically Catholic as she was, Simone was still a Jew. In 1942, during the German occupation of France, she reluctantly fled Europe and sailed to New York with her parents. But she felt like a coward. As soon as they arrived in America she started working on a plan to return to France to join the Resistance. She eventually fled her parents and made it back to London, but she was weak and unwell, and not eating. Simone had always been addicted to fasting, refusing to eat more than the members of some suffering population or another (the children in Indochine, the soldiers on the front, the French during occupation). Not long after arriving in London, when she finally collapsed from exhaustion and was diagnosed with tuberculosis, she kept her illness from her family, and sent happy chatty letters off to America even as she refused food and treatment. She was eventually transferred to a sanitarium, where she died from cardiac failure, caused by semistarvation and tuberculosis, at the age of 34.

Physical Illness?

Anorexia Philosophia?

Suicide-by-Catholicism?

Before we cast poor little Simone into the dustbin of annihilated women also known as saints, we should remember that she was not just any old slave; she was a rebellious slave, a Philosopher Slave! Selfsame as the woman who didn't eat enough, who cringed from human touch, who struggled alongside her comrades in the factory, was the woman who wrote philosophy. A woman who stirred up and recorded her own messy truth, in conversation with a library of brilliant men and their wonderful, terrible ideas. A dust devil.

The rare philosopher exposes herself. Reads and rewrites herself, swimming through, swallowing, pissing into a sea of insightful and dubious texts. The rare philosopher can put fear aside. To those on a different wavelength, the rare philosopher seems jejune in her earnestness and naivete.

I am not sure which I find more disturbing, Simone Weil's ultimate conclusions, or the fact that so many have considered her a saint. If the best moral response to a world of suffering is some form of physical self-destruction, we are really sunk. But if you believe life is a vale of tears, and that a better reality exists beyond the body, it is difficult to construct ethics that affirm life and the material world.

Luckily, Simone was wrong. Refusal of the dominating self does not require denial of the earthly body. Denial of the dominating self is yes-saying to the connected, fragile body, the feminine body, the body of hunger, desire, and vulnerability. It is recognition and acceptance of physical connection and interdependence. Love of the earthly self through love of the earthly other provides the only ethical escape, our only hope.

Simone did see the power of the earthly body, but she could not connect mundane earthly love with God's love. In "The *Iliad* or the Poem of Force," she briefly mentions a world that provides a poignant, painful contrast with oppressive force, "Another world: the faraway, precarious, touching world of peace, of the family" (164). She characterizes that world as a mirage, as unreal. *But that world is real too.* If the world of tenderness and caring is biologically necessary and logically possible, always present but always subject to force, what should we conclude?

How is embodied love able to pick itself up, time and again, to dust itself off and to make itself real?

Simone Weil was an isolated, talented misfit in a world of men. So many writers describe her as homely, but I believe the photos say otherwise. In childhood photos she is radiant and adorable, and in her early twenties there is a revolutionary twinkle in her eye. In the later years she looks increasingly drawn and pasty, like someone who does not take care of herself and who never looks in the mirror (which is in character but ironic, given the depth and brilliance of her self-obsessions). Though the great men of Philosophy are allowed to be funny-looking weirdoes, any woman philosopher can imagine the difficulties faced by someone as strange and brilliant as poor Simone Weil. Biographers mention her "unusual masculine dress," and the fact that she considered it a great misfortune to have been born female (Beauvoir too remarks on Weil's "bizarre outfit"). Her parents often called her Simon, and "our boy." Her resistance to femininity, like her longing for love, is a deeply influential but mostly hidden undercurrent in her work. Attention to that resistance is necessary for understanding how a French woman philosopher from that era who lacked a boyfriend managed to take herself so seriously.

I cannot help but feel something familiar in the character that emerges from the text. Doesn't every female academic have a friend like nerdy, awkward, asexual Simone? I want to take her to the mall, and help her pick out some new clothes. *Simone, you've got to get out into the world. Simone, you've got to eat more—Christ would want you to love the life He gave you. Clean yourself up, girl. Come on, Simone sweetie, let me hold your hand.*

Simone Weil encountered a world that was basically painful, though she saw a shimmering alternative in transcendent pure grace. In an attempt to depict the wretchedness of life (existence framed by force), Weil writes, "Nearly all the *Iliad* takes place far from hot baths. Nearly all of human life, then and now, takes place far from hot baths" (164). But of course that is not true. All that is required for a hot bath is clean water and sunshine, or fire. Much of human life takes place very close to hot baths, nourishing meals, laughter, music, and love, because these things are always present in bodily needs and rhythms, always just around the corner from suffering and war. Where there are no hot baths, the memory of them is what drives us home, or on to a new place. Or onward in the struggle for justice.

Given the centrality of body-hating and self-sacrifice in Weil's philosophical universe it is perhaps not surprising that, outside of religious studies, she has not received much attention from contemporary feminists. Simone Weil certainly does not make a very good feminist hero, but the echoes of her work are resounding. In fact, it can be argued that she is an invisible mother of feminist thought. Iris Murdoch, whose work has deeply shaped feminist philosophy, was a great admirer of Weil. Her last great philosophical work, *Metaphysics as a Guide to Morals*, culminates with a discussion of Weil's ability to "take a firm hold upon the painful reality" of suffering, and to respond with ethics of attention (504).

Weil describes attention as a moral relation not reducible to an act of rational will,

The poet produces the beautiful by fixing his attention something real. It is the same with the act of love. To know that this man who is hungry and thirsty really exists as much as I do—that is enough, the rest follows of itself. The authentic and pure values—truth, beauty and goodness— in the activity of a human being are the result of one and the same act, a certain application of the full attention to the object (Gravity and Grace, 108).

In her description of ethical life as a matter of the direction of energy and loving attention, and in her own commitment to praxis, Weil provides a compelling reference point for feminist philosophy. Ironicially, attention is an ethical response that is individual and intellectual, but it is effective because it is also inherently social and embodied, as any form of true mindfulness is a bodily commitment. Its power lies in its ability to remind of the connections in which we are always already embedded. This is why it is impossible to read Weil without attention to her own tragic body politics.

Sara Ruddick, whose *Maternal Thinking: Toward a Politics of Peace*, is deeply influenced by Weil's concept of attention, describes her own ambivalent response to Simone Weil:

I was repelled by Weil's self-hatred and the anti-Semitism that was one expression of it. Her strenuous, unremitting moral seriousness depressed me. . . . I could barely listen as Weil spoke eloquently of the pain of the oppressed, a pain to which the oppressor must not let herself contribute so much as a gesture, accent, or tone of voice (152).

Michelle Cliff reads Weil through an understanding of internalized racism and female self-denial, experiencing a sense of isolated sisterhood with Weil, and cleaving to her "belief in the power of violence, force, to create and maintain oppression" (324).

Reading Weil may help us gain some understanding not only of oppression, but about how to affirm the body Simone had to deny. It is not better to burn out than to fade away, but how to say yes to a world in which rust never sleeps?

Simone wrote, *In the heart of its inconsolable bitterness . . . if we remain at this point without ceasing to love, we end by touching . . . the central essence, necessary and pure . . . the very love of God.*

I write, Loving the earthly body through its failures. Loving the feminine body: the sick body, the black body, the soft body, the other body, the aging body, the baby body, the fat body, the nonhuman body, the imperfect body, the hurting hungry frightened body. Loving the mighty sea through the storm.

Near the end of her life, Simone spent a lot of time in Harlem. It was her favorite neighborhood in New York, and she loved to wander its streets in the evening, watching the children play. She attended a black Baptist church every Sunday, and described it in a letter to a friend,

> *The religious fervour of the Minister and the congregation explodes into dances much like the Charleston, exclamations, cries, and the singing of spirituals. That's really worth seeing. A true and moving expression of faith, it seems to me (Petrement, 478).*

Simone believed that humans had a basic need for risk, that "the absence of risk produces a type of boredom which paralyses in a different way from fear, but almost as much" (*Need for Roots*, 115). While she was in New York she was obsessed with getting back to France, because she thought she had failed to do her duty—to risk harm for justice. She even tried to get the French government to allow her to parachute into the war front, so she could provide spiritual succor to soldiers.

In his Preface to the 1951 English translation of *The Need for Roots*, T. S. Eliot remarked that it is often difficult to distinguish selflessness and egoism. It is too bad Simone's isolating state of mind prevented her from chilling out in New York for a while. Maybe she could have risked intimacy, and hooked up with a lover at the Baptist church. Someone sensitive and sharp, someone who would have enjoyed the game of opening her up. I'll bet the right person would have found Simone unusually affirming. And perhaps Simone would have found her embodied self, her joyful spirituality, her root chakra. She could have taught her lover the George Herbert poem that she recited as a prayer every day:

> Love bade me welcome; yet my soul drew back,
> Guiltie of lust and sinne.
> But quick-ey'd Love, observing me grow slack
> From my first entrance in,
> Drew nearer to me, sweetly questioning,
> If I lack'd any thing.
> A guest, I answer'd, worthy to be here:
> Love said, You shall be he.
> I the unkinde, ungratefull? Ah my deare,
> I cannot look on thee.
> Love took my hand, and smiling did reply,
> Who made the eyes but I?
> Truth Lord, but I have marr'd them: let my shame
> Go where it doth deserve.
> And know you not, sayes Love, who bore the blame?
> My deare, then I will serve.
> You must sit down, sayes Love, and taste my meat:
> So I did sit and eat.

Perhaps Simone could have found a way to love her own meat.

The Philosopher Queen on War

The Philosopher Queen was sitting on her Brooklyn fire escape in shorts and a down jacket in the middle of October. It was a beautiful fall day and the yellowreds of the brick buildings spoke to the colors of the leaves. But the air was too cold and her calves were in contact with metal.

She thought eating might calm her, and right now she was nervously seeking calm. She'd brought the phone and a stale piece of pbj toast with her when she'd climbed out of the window. Her heart was still beating too fast, and the toast felt like pasty cardboard in her mouth.

Nothing seemed very fun these days. She'd sometimes feel happy around other people, but then she'd brood or get to worrying alone. And weird things kept happening. Like just before, when she was working at the computer, there was a strong smell, unusual and pungent, like gas or something. The smell was so powerful . . . intense . . . and the stove wasn't on. . . .

143

It must be a chemical attack!

Her heart started pounding—she could feel it in her temples as she ran to the window to see if the children in the playground were running to safety, or retching, or keeling over. If there had been some kind of chemical attack, the people in the street would be reacting.

The people in street seemed just fine.

Was it just in her apartment? Was it gone? Had it gotten stronger? *Was she being gassed?*

But who would want to kill *her*?

She sniffed again. She *did* have a headache.

Air! I just need some air! as she opened the window and took a deep breath. Then she grabbed her coat and climbed out.

When had things gotten so strange? She had never been a worry-wort before. Would things ever get back to normal? And why all this sudden interest in normalcy, from a weirdo like her?

The Great Philosophers argued about justifications for entering into war, and over appropriate activities within war. The primary philosophical question about war, since wars appear to be inevitable, is about when it is just to enter into military conflicts against other states. Or in hindsight, to evaluate the morality of wars and military actions. War, then, must be an isolated, definable event with clear boundaries. Those boundaries distinguish the circumstances in which standard moral rules and constraints, such as rules against murder and unprovoked violence, no longer apply. That is why the Great Philosophers stress the importance of good decision-making before wars occur—before the initiation of such special moral events.

But what if war is a pervasive presence in nearly all contemporary life?

Many important questions about war cannot be addressed by an approach that sees war as an event, because war is not just an event. When we think of war as an event, we can only see the need for crisis-based politics and analyses. Then, when the war is over, there is no longer a need for a movement for peace.

A movement against war is a movement against violence, and so requires sustained resistance to the omnipresent violences in our lives.

In a previous season, in the same land but in a very different land, PQ wrote:

> *Los Alamos is burning. The fire was started on purpose, by the National Park Service. A controlled burn that is raging completely out of control, over a huge expanse of high desert that includes the lab on the hill. Less than forty miles from here as the crow flies a huge fire is raging virtually on top of some of the most dangerous radioactive weapons on the planet. The news says there are layers of space and steel and dirt between the bombs and the fire, so I guess shouldn't worry. But still. I am sitting here at ground fucking zero, and I realize it has probably been years since I've really thought about nuclear weapons.*

The lab on the hill had developed the nuclear bombs that America dropped on Japan, technology that had killed thousands in the *flash* of an instant. Now tons and tons of radioactive waste were stored in its miles and miles of beautiful wooded property, former home of Anasazi and Pueblo people. The local economy was still driven by the production of bombs, and the production of knowledge in the service of military power. The lab itself was diverse, employing many local Indians and Hispanics, and quite a few non-American scientists.

> *The air in Santa Fe smells like wood smoke. Floating ash is everywhere. A few deformed birds came by this morning. One red finch had no feathers on the back of her neck, her scruffy scarlet mohawk trembling like a baby buzzard's. I thought I saw an Australian fantail at the feeder, but*

then realized it was a sparrow whose tail had been burned off. Her back arched unnaturally—she must have been in pain—but there was nothing I could give her, no way to help but to fill up the birdbath and to put out more food.

Should we evacuate? There are so many fires raging through New Mexico and Arizona right now, taking to the highway hardly seems like a good idea.

The TV news says that eighty square miles of land has burned, and hundreds of homes have been lost. Streets and streets of houses, just over-taken by fire.

The television is not telling me anything about whether the air is safe or whether the burning trees are releasing stores of radioactive matter. Where are we supposed to get information? Is there something I ought to do?

Hoping for a burst of participatory democracy, the Philosopher Queen assumed her disguise, and went off to a Town Meeting. She appreciated the information the activists and government officials provided about levels of toxins and relief efforts. The scientific facts allowed her to gauge her own safety, and to assess the performance of the institutions that were supposed to keep the community protected and informed.

The man sitting next to PQ had the tweedy look of a physicist. Before the meeting had begun, he'd turned to her and introduced himself as a representative from the lab on the hill. He was there to observe, not to participate.

PQ was intrigued. He seemed like a nice, normal person, and he sat there beside her with his heart and his mind and his penis (she guessed) and his nice brown shoes. She felt an academic affinity, a smart-person connection with him. He sat there beside her with his elbow occasionally touching her arm, with his brain of chemical reactions, with his own abstract models and latent justifications. Just like her. He wanted to be able to do his thing, to seek answers to difficult problems, just like a Philosopher Queen.

She knew at the lab they were developing networks of knowledge, linked systems of computers with distinct areas of expertise. Like linked brains but better, because it was *possible* to link computers. Because computers can fully disclose what they know, and nothing blocks reception of the Other.

Could the Philosopher Queen and the physicist become a linked system? If she turned and kissed him, would he learn the algorithm of the antiwar body? Would she internalize a concern about security that would make her see weapons of mass destruction in a more positive light?

What would it cost to link the scientist and the Philosopher Queen? Who would provide the funding? Would this be the best way to address the crisis at hand?

But what *was* the crisis at hand?

The crisis at hand was a local fire, not the fact that so many tons of radioactive waste were sitting so vulnerably, so nearby, or that forestry management seemed to be failing throughout the American West.

Listening to it all, PQ wrote in her notebook: *A nuclear economy is like a slave economy* and *People can get away with any evil just by claiming that it will provide more jobs.* But she did not bring up those points for discussion in the Town Meeting, or with the scientist sitting next to her. She wondered if there was something she ought to do. She knew nothing much would come of this meeting.

One of the reasons this particular meeting would come to nothing was the fact that the only people who raised challenging questions were the egocentric hypochondriacs who were only worried about themselves, and the ultraparanoids who didn't believe anything anyone told them, except when someone told them that the government was covering up the truth.

I've had this horrible shortness of breath, and a splitting headache ever since those fires started. My portable Geiger counter says radioactivity rates are 7.5, and I don't even know what that means! I can't live with all these unknowns. And there's been a horrible smell, pungent and intense. I have no idea what it is. Would somebody please tell me what to do!

PQ thought of the old cliché: the worst thing about democracy is the people.

How could she have hope for democracy when she found so many of the thoughts and opinions of the general public (them! out there!) to be such stupid crap?

Oh of course all people have the right to their stupid crap, and to express their own stupid crap in whatever form they'd like, as long as they don't hurt anyone else in the process, or prevent others from saying their own stupid crappy stuff. But is that really the full extent of the promise of democracy? The freedom to express crapola? Didn't the Iroquois have something else in mind when they created democracy here so long ago?

The Philosopher Queen believed that education (of a certain sort) was necessary for meaningful democratic participation. Since she'd had the privilege of a good education, she thought she'd put her voice out there.

Dear Editor:

The fire in city of La La La is all over the news right now, but the mainstream media is missing the point. Recent events around La La La Lab, including the manmade wildfire that nearly incinerated a horrifying amount of radioactive materials stored there, show that we can no longer afford the risks of a nuclear war economy.

La la la. Blah blah blah. Her letters never got printed.

∗ ∗ ∗

PQ had been time-traveling through their wars for far too long. She started wearing her own missile defense shield.

∗ ∗ ∗

One provocative claim of the postmodern turn is the belief that everything, including science, is a myth. The negative interpretation of this view is that no method of science or knowledge-seeking is superior to others, and that there is nothing we can truly know. PQ preferred the more positive interpretation, which is that if all forms of knowledge are contingent human creations, much like stories, then we need to know the purpose of a theory in order to evaluate its adequacy. Stories are ways of making sense of the world and our place in it, and stories help justify certain ways of being human over others. If we have the power to claim or create our own stories, or own myths, the question is obvious: What stories do we want to create, to propogate?

The following spring, in the same land but in a different land, the Philosopher Queen looked out and noticed that the far edge of her back fence marked the beginning of a space that was more black and more poor than the block she lived on—the block she faced. She hadn't planned it this way. She'd bought that house because she wanted to live in a racially mixed neighborhood. It's hard to put your finger on what's wrong with gentrification when you're one of the gentry. Either that, or there's nothing wrong with it. You be the judge.

A few months later there were riots in the city, when a cop shot and killed another unarmed man, the fifteenth black man killed by city police, for no reason, really, in just a few years. Protests broke out, and in the city's poorest neighborhoods, the edges of protest turned to rioting.

As she prepared to discuss the *Autobiography of Malcolm X* with her Moral and Political Ideas students, PQ played "Fight the Power" by the Isley Brothers over and over on her cheap office boombox. She thought about Public Enemy's use of the Isley Brothers' lyric, about the relationships between racism and crime, and about how music can be an incredible political force, or a soothing tonic. Even though terrible things were happening in her city, the music lightened her step, and made her want to dance. Was that a sin?

Was that experience something that happened in her mind, or in her body?

PQ was gardening in summer, cutting down renegade vines and cleaning weeds out of the sidewalk cracks, when she came across a crumpled letter in the front yard. She was excited, because the week before she'd found a handout on the proper uses of which and that, a grammatical rule she'd always had a hard time remembering.

Alx,

What's up Dawg. Hows all the gool old boys of the MCK doing. Man, this shit is some hard fucking work. You get no sleep for days at a time. I'm probably doing over 1000 pushups a day. Every morning at 4:30 is P.T. its a 2 hr workout. The worst is if you fuck up. You get a 2hour cycle. That's when they shut all the windows in your Barracks and push your racks back. Put on full outfit and exercise till you pass out. You sweat so much the condesation builds up and water sweats from the ceiling. People go loco every day. My bunkmate wet himself and went AWOL. This one kid in the Barracks next to us was on his 7th week and tried to hang himself.

Even I cried myself to sleep the first week or so. Its hard being away from home.

What made me feel a lot better was when I got a paycheck for 1,200 dollars. Plus the fact in another month and a half I'll be living on the beach in Florida so fuck the Bullshit. Most the cats here are some old style smokers anyways. The Brothers here are a trip. Theres even a Jamaican here but he's a Bitch. He got his ass jumped in the Bathroom. There's a few fags too but they don't try dick. There was this one kid named Compton who screwed up and got us all cycled, man we kicked the shit out of him. Just like Full Metal Jacket. Well, do me a favor and keep an eye on my sweetie for me. If anyone lays a finger on her make sure to let them know I'll be home in a matter of weeks and I'll kick the living fuck out of them. After I'm threw with them you'll need to check Dental records to I.D. the body. When you get your ass beat day after day it tends to turn you into a badass motherfucker. Don't worry though, there's no Brain washing going on, If it was uptown I'd be smoking a blunt right now.

Your nigga,

Keenan

P.S. Tell Hum he'd better fuck Carissa.

Time is really wastin'
There's no guarantee
Smile is in the making
We got to fight the powers that be
Hey baby
Fight the power
Fight
Fight the power

The Philosopher Queen thought: I would love for everything I hate to die. I would love to wield the sword of truth, to eliminate the undesirable, to disappear it all.

Sometimes she even enjoyed causing pain, though she never quite got why. Maybe if she knew more about Afghanistan, she would understand all the other disasters she participated in.

But to really understand the full story, she needed to know about oil, and the reserves lying beneath the beleaguered desert.

And to really understand oil, you've got to understand First World consumption patterns, and the fact that I am so happy when I can just get in my car and drive.

But to really understand what is going on there, you've got to understand how economies work, and why a steady stream of grasping desire is necessary for the accumulation of wealth.

Any good feminist knows you cannot understand economies without really understanding particular forms of family, and patterns of labour distribution.

But of course families depend on women, and we've only begun to understand the many meanings of sex and gender.

To really know what is going on with women in this situation, in this crisis at hand, we have to look at local systems of education. We need to know if Carissa wants to be fucked by Hum, and why women let men get away with so much shit.

We need to know about poverty, and repression, religion, and freedom. To really know what is going on, we need to understand the Reagan-Bush years, the global public health crisis, the fallout of the culture wars, Enron, Haliburton, and the 2000 elections.

Hey! *In order to really get it*, we have to understand everything that makes possible an animal that manufactures its own demise.

PQ felt like she did not understand a damned thing. And the fact that her knowledge was socially constituted, that she was a socially embedded being, and not really a free-floating atom, just did not seem to help.

But if an animal can learn to act contrary to its own basic interests, so against the order of the flesh, then surely it could learn to successfully seek health and flourishing. If an animal could learn to accept so many lies about herself, then surely she could learn to be curious about the unarticulated truth.

The Philosopher Queen met the Priestess of Disks on an airplane. The older, browner woman patted her arm. "Don't take yourself so goddamned seriously, sweetie!" she said as she danced toward the cockpit, the swirling green earth in her left hand and a cell phone in her right.

You are a question, not an answer.

You'll jump when the heat becomes too much to bear.

With every leap you choose your trajectory,
so keep your eye on the curve of the land.

Works Cited

All dictionary definitions are from *Webster's New World Dictionary*, Third College Edition.

The Philosopher Queen

For the birdcage analogy:
Frye, Marilyn. 1983. "Oppression." In *The Politics of Reality: Essays in Feminist Theory*. Freedom, Calif.: The Crossing Press.

War as an Opportunity for Learning

Carson, Rachel. 1962 *Silent Spring.*, Boston: Houghton Mifflin.

Enloe, Cynthia. 2001. *Bananas, Beaches, and Bases: Making Feminist Sense of International Politics*. Berkeley: University of California Press.

Johnson, Chalmers. 2000. *Blowback: The Costs and Consequences of American Empire*. New York: Henry Holt.

Meeks, Ronald L. 2001. *National Science Foundation Division of Science Resource Studies Data Brief.* NSF 02-300, October 9, 2001. www.nsf.gov.

Russell, Bertrand. 1971. *Prevent the Crime of Silence: Report from the Sessions of the International War Crimes Tribunal Founded by Bertrand Russell.* Nottingham, UK: Bertrand Russell Peace Foundation. Full text available at www2.prestel.co.uk/littleton/v1tribun.htm.

Schott, Robin. 1996. "Gender and 'Postmodern' War." *Hypatia* 11(4): 19—29. Also see other articles in this special issue on "Women and Violence."

Thomas, William. 1995. *Scorched Earth: The Military's Assault on the Environment.* Philadelphia: New Society Publishers.

United Nations. 1996. U.N. Resolution 51/210, "Measures to Eliminate International Terrorism," 17 December 1996.

USA-PATRIOT Act (Uniting and Strengthening America by Providing Appropriate Tools Required to Intercept and Obstruct Terrorism Act). 25 October 2001. H.R. 3162.

Watson, Dale L. 2002. "The Terrorist Threat Confronting the United States: Statement before the Senate Select Committee on Intelligence," Washington, D.C., www.fbi.gov/congress/congress02/watson020602.htm.

Critical Theory and the Science of Complexity

Anzaldúa, Gloria. 1987. *Borderlands/La Frontera: The New Mestiza.* San Francisco: Spinsters/Aunt Lute.

Casti, John L. 1994. *Complexification: Explaining a Paradoxical World through the Science of Surprise.* New York: HarperPerennial.

Crenshaw, Kimberle, Neil Gotanda, Garry Peller, and Kendall Thomas, eds. 1996. *Critical Race Theory: The Key Writings That Formed the Movement.* New York: New Press.

Gell-Mann, Murray. 1994. *The Quark and the Jaguar: Adventures in the Simple and the Complex.* New York: W.H. Freeman.

——— and George J. Gumerman, eds. 1994. *Understanding Complexity in the Prehistoric Southwest.* Reading, Mass.: Addison-Wesley.

Midgley, Mary. 1994. *The Ethical Primate: Humans, Freedom, and Morality.* New York: Routledge.

Getting Closer: On the Ethics of Knowledge Production

Keller, Evelyn Fox. 1992. *A Feeling for the Organism: The Life and Work of Barbara McClintock*. San Francisco: W.H. Freeman.

Codeword: Diversity

Lorde, Audre. 1984. "The Master's Tools Will Never Dismantle the Master's House." In *Sister Outsider*. Freedom, Calif.: The Crossing Press.
West, Cornel. 1994. *Race Matters*. New York: Vintage.

Justice, Joy, and Feminist Sex

Bar On, Bat-Ami. 1994. "The Feminist Sexuality Debates and the Transformation of the Political." In *Adventures in Lesbian Philosophy*, ed. Claudia Card. Bloomington: Indiana University Press.
Benhabib, Seyla. 1995. "Subjectivity, Historiography, and Politics: Reflections on the Feminism/Postmodernism Exchange." In *Feminist Contentions: A Philosophical Exchange*, ed. Seyla Benhabib, Judith Butler, Drucilla Cornell, and Nancy Fraser. New York: Routledge.
Chanter, Tina. 1995. *Ethics and Eros: Irigaray Rewrites the Philosophers*. New York: Routledge.
Cornell, Drucilla. 1995. "What Is Ethical Feminism?" In *Feminist Contentions: A Philosophical Exchange*, ed. Seyla Benhabib, Judith Butler, Drucilla Cornell, and Nancy Fraser. New York: Routledge.
Fraser, Nancy. 1995. "Pragmatism, Feminism, and the Linguistic Turn." In *Feminist Contentions: A Philosophical Exchange*, ed. Seyla Benhabib, Judith Butler, Drucilla Cornell, and Nancy Fraser. New York: Routledge.
Lorde, Audre. 1984. "Uses of the Erotic: The Erotic as Power." In *Sister Outsider*. Freedom, Calif.: The Crossing Press.
Lugones, María. 1994. "Purity, Impurity, and Separation." *Signs* 19(2): 458–79.

———. 2003. *Pilgrimages/Peregrinajes: Theorizing Coalition Against Multiple Oppressions*. Lanham: Rowman and Littlefield.

Snitow, Ann, Christine Stansell, Sharon Thompson, eds. 1983. *Powers of Desire: The Politics of Sexuality*. New York: Monthly Review Press.

Willett, Cynthia. 1995. *Maternal Ethics and Other Slave Moralities*. New York: Routledge.

Lesbian and Its Synonyms

Alexander, F. Matthias. 1990. *The Alexander Technique*. New York: Carol Publishing Group.

Bachmann, Mona. 1999. "Queer, Hasbians and Ex-Gays: Post-Lesbian Figures at the Millennium." Unpublished.

Berman, Jennifer, and Laura Berman. 2001. *For Women Only: A Revolutionary Guide to Overcoming Sexual Dysfunction and Reclaiming Your Sex Life*. New York: Henry Holt.

Brant, Beth (Degonwadonti). 1991. *Food and Spirits*. Ithaca, N.Y.: Firebrand Books.

Calhoun, Cheshire. 1995. "The Gender Closet: Lesbian Disappearance under the Sign 'Women.'" *Feminist Studies* 2(1): 7–34.

Califia, Pat. 1994. *Public Sex: The Culture of Radical Sex*. San Francisco: Cleis Press.

Chia, Mantak, and Maneewan Chia. 1986. *Healing Love through the Tao: Cultivating Female Sexual Energy*. Huntington, N.Y.: Healing Tao Books.

Davis, Madeline D., and Elizabeth Lapovsky Kennedy. 1993. *Boots of Leather, Slippers of Gold: The History of a Lesbian Community*. New York: Penguin Books.

Duggan, Lisa. 2000. *Sapphic Slashers: Sex, Violence, and American Modernity*. Durham, N.C.: Duke University Press.

Esterberg, Kristin G. 1997. *Lesbian and Bisexual Identities: Constructing Communities, Constructing Selves*. Philadelphia: Temple University Press.

Frye, Marilyn. 1983. "To Be and Be Seen." In *The Politics of Reality*. Trumansburg, N.Y.: Crossing Press.

Moraga, Cherríe. 1983. *Loving in the War Years: Lo Que Nunca Paso por Sus Labios*. Boston: South End Press.

Summerscale, Kate. 1998, *The Queen of Whale Cay: The Eccentric Story of "Joe" Carstairs, Fastest Woman on Water*. New York: Viking Penguin.

Weeks, Laurie. 1995. "Debbie's Barium Swallow." In *The New Fuck You: Adventures in Lesbian Reading*, ed. Liz Kotz and Eileen Myles. New York: Semiotext(e).

Wittig, Monique. 1986. *The Lesbian Body*. Boston: Beacon Press.

Reading Simone Weil: It's Better to Fade Away

Cliff, Michelle. 1993. "Sister/Outsider: Some Thoughts on Simone Weil." In *Between Women: Biographers, Novelists, Critics, Teachers and Artists Write about Their Work on Women*, ed. Carol Ascher, Louise DeSalvo, and Sara Ruddick. New York: Routledge.

McLellan, David. 1990. *Utopian Pessimist: The Life and Thought of Simone Weil*. New York: Poseidon Press.

Miles, Sian. 1986. *Simone Weil: An Anthology*. New York: Grove Press.

Murdoch, Iris. 1992. *Metaphysics as a Guide to Morals*. New York: Penguin Books.

Nye, Andrea. 1994. *Philosophia: The Thought of Rosa Luxemburg, Simone Weil, and Hannah Arendt*. New York: Routledge.

Petrement, Simone. 1976. *Simone Weil: A Life*. New York: Schocken Books.

Ruddick, Sara. 1993. "New Combinations: Learning from Virginia Woolf." In *Between Women: Biographers, Novelists, Critics, Teachers and Artists Write about Their Work on Women*, ed. Carol Ascher, Louise DeSalvo, and Sara Ruddick. New York: Routledge.

Weil, Simone. 2001. *Gravity and Grace*. New York: Routledge.

———. 1952. *The Need for Roots*. London: Routledge and Kegan Paul.

———. 1951. *Waiting for God*. New York: G. P. Putnam's Sons.

———. 1986. "Analysis of Oppression" (from "Reflections Concerning the Causes of Liberty and Social Oppression"). In *Simone Weil: An Anthology*, ed. Sian Miles. New York: Grove Press.

———. 1986. "Human Personality." In *Simone Weil: An Anthology*, ed. Sian Miles. New York: Grove Press.

———. 1986. "*The Iliad*, or The Poem of Force." In *Simone Weil: An Anthology*, ed. Sian Miles. New York: Grove Press.

Index